P R A I S E   F O R

H<u>EAVE</u>N

At a time when we are surrounded by so much despair, Daniel Brown pulls back the curtain to give us an unencumbered view of the hope that is heaven.

Debby Boone
SINGER AND AUTHOR
SHERMAN OAKS, CALIFORNIA

"Let heaven fill your thoughts. Do not think only about things down here on earth" (Col. 3:2, *NLT*). *Heaven* helps us to do just that, shedding scriptural light on a subject we need to spend more time thinking about. This book is exciting!

Dr. Bill Bright
FOUNDER AND PRESIDENT, CAMPUS CRUSADE FOR CHRIST INTERNATIONAL
ORLANDO, FLORIDA

When I see the name Daniel Brown on an article, tape or book, I've come to excitedly expect (and appreciate) clear thinking articulated through a loving pastor's heart. *Heaven* does not disappoint!

Todd Hunter
NATIONAL DIRECTOR, ASSOCIATION OF VINEYARD CHURCHES
ANAHEIM, CALIFORNIA

At last, a travel guide to my favorite destination! This book touched me in a special way. Daniel Brown is a faithful pastor, leader, teacher and communicator.

Rev. Isaac J. Stiles, Jr.
CONGREGATION SUPPORT GROUP COORDINATOR
LOS ANGELES SOUTHERN BAPTIST ASSOCIATION
DOWNEY, CALIFORNIA

WHAT THE BIBLE REVEALS ABOUT

HEAVEN

Answers to Your Questions

DANIEL A. BROWN, Ph.D.

Regal

A Division of Gospel Light
Ventura, California, U.S.A.

Publisned by Regal Books
A Division of Gospel Light
Ventura, California, U.S.A.
Printed in U.S.A.

Regal Books is a ministry of Gospel Light, an evangelical Christian publisher dedi-
cated to serving the local church. We believe God's vision for Gospel Light is to provide church leaders with biblical, user-friendly materials that will help them evan-
gelize, disciple and minister to children, youth and families.

It is our prayer that this Regal book will help you discover biblical truth for your
own life and help you meet the needs of others. May God richly bless you.

For a free catalog of resources from Regal Books/Gospel Light please contact your Christian
supplier or call 1-800-4-GOSPEL.

All Scripture quotations, unless otherwise indicated, are taken from the NASB—New
American Standard Bible, © 1960, 1962, 1963, 1968, 1971, 1972, 1973, 1975, 1977 by The
Lockman Foundation. Used by permission.

The other version used is:
NIV—The Holy Bible, New International Version®. NIV®. Copyright © 1973, 1978, 1984 by
International Bible Society. Used by permission of Zondervan Publishing House. All
rights reserved.

Cover design by Kevin Keller
Interior design by Rob Williams
Edited by Deena Davis

Library of Congress Cataloging-in-Publication Data
Brown, Daniel Alan, 1953–
    Heaven / Daniel A. Brown.
      p.   cm.
    Includes bibliographical references.
    ISBN 0-8307-2341-2
    1. Heaven—Christianity. I. Title.
BT846.2.B78   1999   99-15625
236'.24—dc21   CIP

2 3 4 5 6 7 8 9 10 11 12 13 14 15 / 05 04 03 02 01 00

Rights for publishing this book in other languages are contracted by Gospel Literature
International (GLINT). GLINT also provides technical help for the adaptation, translation and publishing of Bible study resources and books in scores of languages world-
wide. For further information, contact GLINT, P.O. Box 4060, Ontario, CA 91761-1003,
U.S.A., or the publisher. You may also send E-mail to Glintint@aol.com, or visit their
website at www.glint.org.

To Phil Osselaer,
Greatly respected and deeply loved
on earth, yet
Expected and loved even more
in Heaven.
Thank you for teaching us
how to die.

CONTENTS

In My Father's house are many dwelling places; if it were not so, I would have told you; for I go to prepare a place for you. And if I go and prepare a place for you, I will come again, and receive you to Myself; that where I am, there you may be also.

JESUS OF NAZARETH (JOHN 14:2,3)

For I delivered to you as of first importance what I also received, that Christ died for our sins according to the Scriptures, and that He was buried, and that He was raised on the third day according to the Scriptures.... And if Christ has not been raised, your faith is worthless; you are still in your sins. Then those also who have fallen asleep in Christ have perished. If we have hoped in Christ in this life only, we are of all men most to be pitied.

PAUL OF TARSUS (1 CORINTHIANS 15:3,4,17-19)

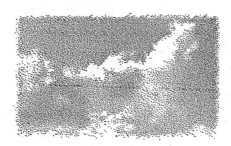

F O R E W O R D

There are two reasons I am thankful for this book. The first is rooted in forty years of pastoral experience; the second is very subjective and personally moving.

First, as pragmatic as life forces us to be, and as important as it is to learn maturity in dealing with life's duties, problems and relationships, my lifetime as a shepherd of souls has verified this: The ultimate point of human inquiry isn't *this life* but the *afterlife*. An in-wrought awareness of our eternal significance has been inscribed there by our Creator.

C. S. Lewis observed the human temptation to intellectualize vanity, and the emptiness issuing from any human pursuit of the mind that is unaccompanied by a nurturing of the spirit. He described "people without chests, whose hearts have atrophied." That thought readily comes to mind when we view today's society—a culture that usually perceives itself as educationally and technologically advanced, even as it continues to shrivel within for want of spiritual substance.

It isn't as though the "spiritual" is not pursued; it is simply sought in all the wrong places: everything from self-help, do-it-yourself books on spirituality to 900 numbers proffering the promise of psychic counseling to "tune your soul to the stars." All become fodder for faith-hungry seekers after truth. Sadly, the end result is either delusion or despair—the inevitable confusion of the soul due to swallowing the swill of demonic philosophies or buying into Eastern mysticism mellow-marketed by hip, westernized New Age gurus.

The most common denominator of these "old age with new face" systems is their notions about Heaven. They may focus on everything from improving your view of yourself to pursuing the preservation of earth's environment, but the bottom line is they *must* deal with Heaven if they want to seriously consider our human condition and destiny. Therefore, any honest look at the subject forces the inquirer to the Holy Scriptures of the Old and New Testaments.

So, decades of pastoral experience make me grateful for this book. Dr. Daniel Brown's work draws us to the one Sourcebook that elaborates on Heaven with authority. No one exegetes Heaven like its Builder, and no one can open our understanding to its promise more clearly than the One who said, "I go to prepare a place for you." As these pages lead you on a practical, insightful, intellectually satisfying and spiritually meaningful tour of God's intended "forever home," you will be brought to a place of hope built on substance and of promise undergirded by reality. Yes, pastorally speaking, I am glad to commend this book to you. But there is a deep *personal* gratification as well.

Daniel Brown and his dear wife Pamela have been beloved friends for decades, since the time they were students at UCLA and Anna and I were the thirty-something pastors of a church just beginning to explode with growth. During the growth of The Church On The Way, the Browns became a part of our pastoral team. As the years have passed, it has been such a delight to witness the remarkable growth of their ministry and influence in the Church across the nation and elsewhere. The fact that Daniel graciously refers to me as a "spiritual father" to him moves me, and that they both treat Anna and me as their third set of parents is equally dear to us.

The pastoral and the personal make this book a double joy. First, because it will be such a valuable resource to many, and second, because it is such a happy achievement to witness from the hands of "one of our kids." That may seem like a glib remark to describe a studied scholar and doctor of philosophy, but there's no hint of immaturity here—only love and gratitude.

Read on. You're going to love what follows...and I believe you're going to be very grateful, too.

Jack W. Hayford

SENIOR PASTOR, THE CHURCH ON THE WAY
PRESIDENT, THE KING'S SEMINARY
LOS ANGELES, CALIFORNIA
MAY 1999

I N T R O D U C T I O N

No greater promise has ever been made than Jesus' pledge to grant His followers life after death in Heaven. To verify His ability to make good on that offer, He rose from the dead after being crucified on a cross outside of Jerusalem nearly two thousand years ago. Ever since He ascended back into the heavens, passing through a cloud and out of sight, His followers have been awaiting His return (see Acts 1:9-11). While waiting, many have "fallen asleep" and died. But Jesus said,

> "I am the resurrection and the life; he who believes in Me shall live even if he dies" (John 11:25).

Life after death—what does the Bible tell us about Heaven and about what happens to us after we leave this life on Earth? What exactly did Jesus mean about living even if we die? What will our life after this life be like?

Our culture is permeated with speculation about life after death. Movies like *What Dreams May Come* promise that Heaven is more wonderful and fantastic than almost anything we can imagine in this life, with colors and possibilities that defy earthly limitations. Heaven is what you want it to be, with no rules and no judgments. But the picture such movies paint about Heaven almost always has a catch that makes Heaven seem less than perfectly desirable (i.e., it is lonely without our earthly love). God is usually out of the picture or at least not in the center of Heaven. The primary focus in Heaven belongs not to God, but to humans, whose love, courage or refusal to give up enables them to transcend all limitations—earthly or heavenly.

A quick pass through bookstores will reveal people's interest in near-death experiences and their fascination with *spirit-beings*. Hypnotists, journalists and psychiatrists pass along their anecdotal evidence about what lies beyond the veil. They depict death as a pleasant journey toward shimmering lights and flowered meadows. In dying can be found the real meaning for life, we are told. Angels are popularly portrayed as benevolent guides or special-assignment protectors of people, who intervene at the right moment in order to teach humans some lesson. In *It's a Wonderful Life*, angels earn their wings by mentoring humans about life choices.

These cultural views of Heaven, life after death and spirit-beings include small bits of biblical imagery—just enough to mislead people into thinking that the pictures are mostly accurate. But they also communicate profoundly unbiblical notions like reincarnation. No wonder most believers are unclear about many of the specifics of Heaven; it is hard to maintain a biblical picture of Heaven in the face of so many other stories and philosophies about it. Most Christians have a collage of heavenly images, but not all of the pictures have been cut from the pages of the Bible.

The few intriguing facts the Bible presents to us about life after death are scattered throughout several passages, leaving most readers with only sketchy details and a partial picture of what awaits us after this life. More than we would like to acknowledge, the Church at large succumbs to common myths and misunderstandings that come from a simplistic, pseudospiritual view of Heaven. We miss incredible opportunities to comfort our friends or loved ones with the specific promises of *eternity* as spelled out in the Scriptures.

Christians confuse *Hades* with *hell*, Heaven with the entire *spirit* world that surrounds the physical world, and *the new heavens and earth* with the existing cosmos. They are puzzled by Paul's reference to the *third heaven*. They are unsure of what it means to be "caught up" into the air to meet Jesus (when the dead "precede" the living), where people like Abraham and David, or Jezebel and Goliath went when they died. It is disconcerting to read in the book of Revelation that the pearl gates and streets of gold are actually in a city *on* the new earth—not *in* the sky, perched on a large cloud.

In order to answer the simple question—What happens to me when I die?—we will have to reacquaint ourselves with the whole picture of creation as it is outlined in the Bible. That means we will talk about places like the *three heavens, Sheol* and the *new earth.* We will also redefine some basic terms *(death, the cloud of witnesses, rebirth, the lake of fire, body)* and review many relevant Bible passages—not just the few that get quoted at funerals and memorial services—about the life that awaits us.

This book builds a systematic yet simple understanding that explains the incredible physical and spiritual realities of our promised afterlife. The reason most of us get confused about the particulars of Heaven is that we try to understand it without understanding the rest of God's work in creation. That is like a young math student trying to understand division without first learning subtraction. As tempting as it is to jump ahead to Heaven, we have many fascinating truths to explore before we get there. Think of this book as a primer on Heaven. Its incremental building-block approach will enable you to receive answers to the specific, personal questions you have about life after death.

For instance, most people want to know:

- Are we reincarnated?
- What will Heaven be like?
- Do we go into limbo—a period of suspended animation—after we die?
- Do we have guardian angels?
- Why did Jesus descend into Hades after His crucifixion?
- Will we recognize our loved ones in Heaven?
- Do near-death experiences tell us anything about Heaven?
- What will we do in Heaven?
- Will there be rewards in Heaven?

At the beginning of each chapter you will find questions about Heaven or other subjects related to life after death. Those questions are answered in each chapter, and they form the building blocks upon which the appendix—the section you may find yourself wanting to read first—is built. It only takes a few moments of personal reflection to realize that the few facts and ideas we have about Heaven do not fit together very well. It is not that we know nothing about the subject; it is that what we do know (or think we know) does not seem to piece together in a coherent fashion.

We are left with a puzzle or, at the least, a few pieces of a puzzle. When we only have some of the pieces of a jigsaw puzzle, we're not able to connect many of them. It takes other pieces to fit together the ones we hold so that a larger picture emerges. The full picture of Heaven is far grander than we could ever construct here on Earth, and the Bible does offer us more than the few puzzle pieces most people carry around with them.

Heaven is our hoped-for reward—the place of great peace and promise, where death and pain no longer have any dominion. It is where we will be able to live out God's perfect plan for us, a pattern for life that continuously fulfills and satisfies our deepest, purest longings. It is life after this life, life after death. We will look at some of the fantastic realities of Heaven that await us and how each of us can know with certainty if we will arrive there.

If you must, read the last chapter—the appendix—first. Then begin the marvelous process of spilling all the puzzle pieces out onto the table and piecing them back together.

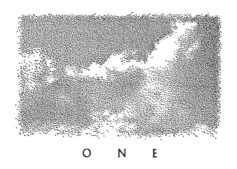

O N E

ETERNITY IN OUR HEARTS

Why do we think about eternity?

What makes Heaven so difficult to picture?

Do pets go to Heaven?

Everyone wants to know what happens when they die. Questions about the afterlife usually come up in childhood when we lose a pet. I was six when my dog Sputnik was hit by my school bus. Talk about a double trauma! We conducted a funeral in the field behind our house, and all I remember is asking my dad if Sputnik was in Heaven.

He fibbed and said, "Yes."

Since then I, too, have told many kids that their beloved pets ended up in Heaven. How can you tell a teary-eyed eight-year-old that her hamster is gone forever? Profound and exacting theological subtleties of the difference between the human soul, which is temporarily housed in a dusty tabernacle, and the mere breath of animals who do not bear the resemblance of God are completely lost on a child who just wants to know that Millie the hamster is happy and fine (i.e., "Will God remember to feed her?").

The child's love for Millie has bestowed both a name and a personality on the cuddly thing. Try telling the little girl that Millie has no soul, no spirit.

Mercifully, she forgets about Millie in a few days, and the great theological question about where Millie will spend eternity becomes moot. Somehow, I know that I am forgiven for having led her astray with my theologically false assurances. By the time she realizes that I lied to her, she will be old enough to understand why.

I grew up believing in Heaven. Even before Sputnik was run over, I had come to believe that Heaven was "up there" somewhere. Perhaps I learned it from my older brother when I was four, the day we climbed up the trellis on our back porch. Our mother happened to come out the back door in time to catch us on the way up.

"What are you doing!?" she demanded.

My brother replied, "Going up to visit God."

To this day I'm not sure if my brother was an early developing theologian or just a quick thinker. In either case, his answer saved us from certain punishment. That day I learned the right answer: Heaven is "up there" somewhere.

A CHILD'S VIEW OF HEAVEN

My theology of Heaven was simple. Good pets (i.e., the ones we love) and good people (same definition) go to Heaven "up there" when they die. And what a place! The streets were made of gold—probably because of all the treasures people had laid "up there." Heaven had pearly gates; I never exactly figured out what "pearly" meant, but I pictured massive white wrought-iron gates.

To me, Heaven was like Disneyland. My family always went to the Magic Kingdom twice a year because we lived in Southern California. We arrived long before the park opened, and each time I was gripped by an unspeakable feeling of excitement and anticipation as I waited for the gates to open. My childhood logic reasoned that the best job in the world would be to work at Disneyland because you could get in before it opened. That is why I envied Saint Peter. He stood at the pearly gates in "Disneyheaven." He got to get in before the rest of us. Whenever I did end up in Heaven, I planned to establish enough seniority to eventually get a job at the gates, so I could watch the new arrivals while they waited in line.

My understanding of Heaven was beginning to take shape: I would die, go "up there" somewhere, wait in line for a while and eventually get into a fabulously fun place. Just as Disneyland had various sections (Frontierland, Fantasyland, Tomorrowland), so did Heaven. Depending on what you liked to do, there were mansions situated on fishing ponds, golf courses, shopping malls, gardens. Everyone and their hamsters and dogs would be having a great time.

There seemed to be only one drawback to Heaven: I would have to meet great-uncles and old aunts who had died long ago before I was born. I worried that they would smell like mothballs, and I would have to hug them and answer their questions. Even though I knew eternity was a long time, I did not relish the prospect of wasting any of it with old people who did not want to ride the Matterhorn of Heaven.

On the other hand, it would be neat to meet all the famous guys from the Bible. I wondered how closely my visual image of Moses would match the real thing. I pictured him with a really long, full white beard and a staff in his hand. It never occurred to me that the staff had long since disintegrated into dust here on Earth; there is no transporter room like on "Star Trek" that allows people to take physical things with them when they go to Heaven.[1]

I was also interested in meeting the lady who drove the tent peg through General Sisera's head.[2] She seemed like quite a lady to my preadolescent mind. I wondered if the peg would be on display in a museum of Bible artifacts. Maybe we would even get to watch studio reenactments of great Bible episodes—parting the Red Sea (then drowning the soldiers), walking on water and so on. That would make Heaven like a combination of Universal Studios and Disneyland. Nothing could be better than that!

Though I thought highly of Heaven throughout my childhood, I did not think about it often. Someone else had to mention Heaven before I gave it more than a passing thought. I figured it was for old people—either those who were old or those who had lived in olden times. I was neither. That is why I supposed Heaven only meant something after you die.

When Gramps Died

In sixth grade I had to think about Heaven quite a bit because my grandfather died. My other grandfather had died when my dad was only 16, so I didn't know him; he was one of those old people I'd have to meet and talk to in Heaven. But my Gramps— I knew him well. He taught me how to shoot a 20-gauge shotgun (only at blue jays, because they rob other birds' nests, and at cans). He was the one who introduced me to coffee even though he claimed it would stunt my growth.

Gramps died of diabetes and a broken heart. At least that's what the grown-ups whispered. I learned later in my life that he had just remodeled his house in the Santa Cruz mountains to get ready to host his cousins from Sweden. Heavy rains caused a tree to fall in such a way that it diverted the water rushing down the hillside right into his and Gram's house. They escaped out a back window just before the whole house slipped down the mountain.

The next day he and Gram walked back to the ruins of their house. Gramps was so anxious that he walked on up ahead. Gram found him on the dirt road with all the life gone out of him. I figured he broke his heart when he fell on the road. All I knew at the time about diabetes was that you could not have sugar on your cereal. That seemed worse to me than mud sliding down a hill and destroying a house.

I remember missing Gramps very much. It seemed really weird to think that I would never see him again. He didn't talk a lot, because he was from Sweden and he never quite mastered English—especially the dialect spoken by boys like me. I was used to silence around him, but the stillness and finality surrounding him now was different. I did not like it.

That was the first time any negative associations attached themselves to my concept of Heaven. Even though I knew Gramps was "happier and in a better place" (which is what everybody said) and that he now could have sugar on his Wheaties and Cheerios, I still wished I could visit him in the mountains and eat out on the deck as we strained to hear the *cawww-caww* of the blue jays.

Someone explained to me that God had been missing Gramps, too. Since I only spent some of my vacations with Gram and Gramps, I suppose I imagined that God got to be with Gramps at other times. I felt a bit cheated that the little time I had with him was now gone. It was not until years later that I began to understand grieving from God's perspective.

I am not sure if I mourned Gramps's death very well. It was confusing to see everyone crying one moment and then telling funny stories about Gramps and laughing the next moment. Years later I came to realize that the best grieving is the roller-coaster ride that takes our emotions up with happy memories, down with the vacant feeling of loss and around with awkwardly decreasing feelings of disorientation and disbelief. Grieving is as much about us as it is about the one who died. But I knew none of that then. I just missed Gramps.

Sixth grade happened to be the year I attended a Billy Graham crusade in Los Angeles. I felt like Mr. Graham was talking directly to me; and when he invited people from all over the stadium to come down and let Jesus forgive their sins, I stood and walked right past my folks and all my relatives, down a million steps to the grass. I wanted my sins forgiven so I could go to Heaven like Gramps.

The crusade workers must have thought I was there with an adult because no one asked or told me anything. I noticed they were giving out little booklets to people, so I asked for one of my own. It was on the Gospel of John. It had some questions to answer like church homework or something. I took that book home and studied all the questions for the next several weeks. Praying, and reading the Bible, got me thinking lots about God and Heaven and Gramps. He used to read his Swedish Bible almost every night.

No More Disneyheaven

Around that same time in my life, my "visions of Glory" changed with prolonged adolescent mental reflection. I reasoned that Heaven probably was not like Disneyland after all, because the adults who had died and gone to Heaven would certainly out-number the kids there by a huge margin. If a vote was taken on what everyone wanted most for Heaven to be like, not many adults like Gramps would pick Disneyland. The adults in Heaven would probably just want to talk or something boring like that. Heaven seemed more serious to me at that time in my life—and more spiritual.

The strange thing was that I could not picture much about it anymore. No one described it to me, not even Rev. Miller in his sermons. I would have stopped drawing on the bulletin with the little pencil that was always on the pew next to the hymnal and sat still if he had told me about what Heaven looked like. He never did; he just said it was a better place. Thus far in my spiritual journey, I had only been able to collect three facts about Heaven: (1) God and Jesus are there, (2) you only go there after you die, and (3) you meet up with lots of people you used to know on Earth when you were alive.

Gramps was the only person I had known who was in Heaven. That kept Heaven very personal and intimate to me. As the weeks and months passed, so too did my thoughts about Heaven. They receded to the edges of my busy and fun life. I derived a certain measure of calmness and peace from knowing that whatever Heaven was, I was going there. That simple faith probably did more than I realize to shape my early life, but the distinctives and particulars of Heaven never registered with me.

"Up There" Somewhere

It was not until high school that Heaven came back to my consciousness in a big way. During my junior year, a buddy of mine was killed in a motorcycle accident (I will not ride on one to this day). Mike Carraher had been one of my best friends before he moved away to Virginia a year before the accident. That made his death seem all the more strange and unreal to me.

We probably never would have seen each other again anyway—except perhaps at our 20-year high school reunion. But since we would not have graduated from the same school, even that was unlikely. A good friend whom I would never see again (because he moved away) was not the same as a good friend who had died. Death changed how I thought about Mike. It felt so final and empty and wrong. It made the memory of him different.

The problem was that I could not picture someone in Heaven. I had seen pictures of the state of Virginia, and I knew where it was on a map. Mike had bearings in my mind when he was still alive, but once he died, I had a hard time imagining where he was. Nothing in my life experience allowed me to mentally frame existence beyond the grave. So, in a weird way, Mike disappeared like someone who gets lost in a big crowd of people. I guessed he was out there or "up there" somewhere, but I could not put it all together in my mind.

Maybe because I was so close to Gramps, I could easily picture myself talking quietly with him as if he were alive. But I could not really have those sorts of chats with a guy who was just a high school buddy, and a goof-off at that.

Believing in Heaven is not the same as being able to visualize it. Doubting Thomas exclaimed, "Seeing is believing!" upon feeling the holes in Jesus' hands. Jesus said, "On the contrary, blessed are [congratulations are in order to] those who believe without seeing."[3] I believed Gramps was in Heaven, and I had no reason to suspect that Mike was not. I believed I would go to Heaven, too. That way of thinking seemed like the most normal thing in the world. But believing in and expecting to go to Heaven did not help me to know what Heaven would really be like.

I suspect that most people believe in some sort of heaven or afterlife. If the world's religions are any indication, regardless of their belief system, everyone but the most cynical expects to go to eternity in some conscious fashion. Life after death fascinates and frightens us. Few of us can conceive of not existing—of simply passing into oblivion. One of the most universal and enduring literary conventions found in poems and novels is the death-rebirth motif (e.g., fall leaves becoming spring flowers). The same is true in most religions. For instance, the belief system of reincarnation teaches that the soul outlives the death of any one of its given lives. The ultimate goal for each soul is to escape the "wheel of samsara"—the unending repetition of the birth-life-death cycle.

It sounds poetically pleasing to talk about endless cycles of life or a phoenix rising from death's ashes. Some philosophers, like Plato, hold the doctrine that the immortal soul exists separately from the body, both before birth and after death. Poets like Wordsworth write of the "indomitableness of the spirit within"[4] that acts as a hint, an intimation, of immortality and "the faith that looks through death."[5] Such writings make for marvelous reading on a quiet rainy day, and they offer interesting discussion at a dinner party. But such perspectives lose their beauty when a dear friend, a beloved companion or an 11-year-old boy haltingly measure out the last couple thousand breaths left to them on Earth.

We need more than poetry and philosophy when our older sister is dying of cancer.

WHAT WE KNOW WITHOUT BEING TOLD

God has set eternity in our hearts[6] so that everyone longs for a forever state. This "eternity" (the Hebrew word *olam*, from the root word meaning "veiled from sight") is like the vanishing point on the horizon—we know it's there, but it remains beyond our reach. Stretching "out of mind," both into the distant past

---

Eternity dwarfs our earthly life span, yet it also magnifies and dignifies our days with the undeniable suggestion of our continued existence.

---

and into the forever future, eternity dwarfs our earthly life span, yet it also somehow magnifies and dignifies our days with the undeniable suggestion of our continued existence. Don Richardson's compelling book *Eternity in Their Hearts* supplies anthropological evidence that every culture has an innate sense of the eternal, put there by God.

No matter how philosophical we become, death strikes us as wrong except in cases where the wasting, agonizing throes of death have come upon a person long before their body gives out completely. Instinctively we know that life is more than merely breathing, more than just staying bodily alive enough to see another day. When all hope is lost of life ever getting better, when all that can be looked forward to is increasing pain and deterioration, something dies inside people that makes continued life its own sort of death.

Proponents of assisted suicide and those people who want us to accept death as a natural, not-to-be-feared by-product of life rely on the argument that life is defined by quality of days, not just quantity of days. While they are wrong to take upon themselves the awful decision of who should die, they are correct in seeing life as more than merely a string of successive days.

Eternity is a quality of life, not just an endless duration of any kind of life. What we long for is not just living forever. What resonates deep in our hearts is a sincere expectation of someday enjoying a life of perpetual good and bounty. That is not a fanciful pipe dream! It is a foreshadowing of Heaven. It is what this book is all about.

We were meant to live forever. That is what God intended.

We know this deep in our souls. But the knowing and the wanting do not reveal anything to us about eternal life in Heaven. We want to know what it will be like. In our desire to know more about the place where we will spend eternity, we are like kids anticipating a great summer vacation.

I can remember as a seven-year-old child the first time I really looked forward to something I could hardly imagine. My dad promised to take us fishing on our big camping trip throughout the western states. We got ready for the big happening by buying some cheap starter-set fishing poles for me and my older (theologian) brother. We tied heavy rubber weights to the end of the line, and I practiced casting and retrieving for hours in the street in front of our house. I got so good at casting my line that I could hit anyplace on the street or in the Toppings's front yard across the way.

I pretended to reel in big fish. Some big ones even got away, so that it seemed more lifelike. I had never been to the Grand Teton National Park in Wyoming, standing next to a swirling, rushing river, casting my line from amid boulders and brush. The first fish

I ever caught was nothing like I had imagined back on the curb by our driveway. The sky was bigger and bluer; the sound of the cascading water and bubbles was deafening; the thrill and screams were real; the tug on my pole was so sudden and captivating.

Nothing in the sports store where we bought the poles, nothing in my make-believe casting and catching of fish in the street, nothing in my imagination came even close to the rush of sights and sounds and sensations that spun around like a fast-moving kaleidoscope when I caught my first fish. How banal a street-cast became the instant I experienced the real thing in that Wyoming gorge.

The same God who put the awareness of eternity in our hearts did so in such a way as to keep us from figuring out all its particulars on our own, because Heaven is not made of the same stuff as this world. None of our natural senses can perceive it. Lots of people have their own images of what it will be like—in the same way I pictured Disneyland and the big white gate. But Heaven cannot be imagined from our end of things. Many sincere people go wrong in their visualizations of Heaven because they forget that God has in mind for them something very different from what they can conceive of on their own.

In fact, that is exactly what the Bible tells us:

No eye has seen, no ear has heard, no mind has conceived what God has prepared for those who love him (1 Corinthians 2:9, *NIV*).

What we can count on is that Heaven will be much better than what we could imagine on our own. That is hard for us to believe because we can't imagine anything better than we can imagine! The Bible tells us that God can do exceedingly more than we can ask or think.[7]

WHAT WE CAN'T KNOW UNTIL WE'RE THERE

It reminds me of a day when I was exposed to a way of life very different from my own. A pastor friend of mine was unable to play a round of golf that had been set up with a very wealthy member of his church, so he invited me to take his place. As a novice golfer, I was thrilled but a bit nervous to take my cheap set of clubs to a posh country club where the clubhouse workers loaded them onto the golf cart for me. Throughout the round of golf, our caddie told us what clubs to use and where to place our putts—not that such advice meant anything to my erratic game.

I was actually relieved to be finished with the round because I felt so out of place. When I took off my Kmart-special golf shoes, a worker took them from me; I figured they were not high-enough quality for the course, and I would be fined a throwaway fee. Imagine my surprise when they were returned to me—cleaned, polished and sealed in a plastic bag!

My host told me not to worry about my shoes or my clubs they would be loaded into our car after lunch. We went into the clubhouse and sat at a nicely set table. I waited for a menu, but my host seemed unconcerned at the poor service. Five minutes later a waiter came to take our orders. Only then did my host explain that there were no menus; you could order anything you wanted. Period. I mentally froze. Here was my chance to order any delicacy, from lobster tail to stroganoff, and all I could think of was a cheeseburger and fries.

Just think how dull our vision for Heaven is compared to what God has in mind for us. God has better, more wonderful things prepared for us, so He takes care of the ordering. Heaven will be wonderful beyond imagining.

Heaven is "wonderful" in the purest sense of the word. I don't mean just great and fabulous, but strange, extraordinary, incomprehensible—like nothing seen before. It is what the angel said of his name ("Why do you ask my name, seeing it is wonderful?") when Manoah, a Danite, wanted to know more about him as a messenger of God.[8] Manoah wanted to offer the angel a meal of goat; the angel told Manoah to offer a sacrifice to the Lord instead.

"Wonderful" means "miraculous" and "otherworldly"— something that causes us to feel awe. It describes things for which we have no earthly context, no way to understand them within the physical laws that govern our natural world. That is what makes our earthly ideas about Heaven so inadequate. It is understandable—and touching—to locate Heaven "in your heart" or to say "Heaven is to the right of your dreams, to the left of your wishes." But we know it's not true. There must be more to it than that. If Heaven is merely in the hearts of everyone who loves us, and we go to live in their memories after we die, then our eternity only lasts for a generation or two. No one holds their great-great-great-grandmother in their heart.

Reducing the wonderful reality of Heaven to earthly sentiment is one of the most common misperceptions in our culture. Heaven is not anywhere and anything we want it to be; it is far beyond any of our earthly imaginings. That is why we must turn to the Bible to gain a perspective on eternity.

A Different Sense of Time

We are so accustomed to viewing matters from our own perspective that it's easy to lose sight of the fact that our world is a mere shadow of the reality that lies beyond the reach of our physical senses.[9] Just as it is difficult for a youngster to grasp that there were people and a world long before the child existed, it is hard for people to fathom the reality of the source from which our "reality" came.

According to the Bible, "the worlds were prepared by the word of God, so that what is seen was not made out of things which are visible."[10] When God spoke, the worlds were instantly framed. From the realm of His eternal, spiritual existence, God called our physical world into being in the midst of nothingness.[11] The world that we see is very real and not, as Plato taught, a mere appearance of the ideal form in the heavens. Its substance and form were, at a moment in time, created; they have not always existed in the same manner that God has always existed.

Western culture generally views time as a linear progression that moves forward in measurable units. Most Eastern cultures see time as a repetitive series of cycles like the seasons, winding their way on and on. In either case, people tend to view life in a fairly egocentric way; we imagine that the life we now know is the beginning point from which every other life is to be seen. This is a major stumbling block when it comes to getting a better understanding of Heaven. By looking forward in time, wondering how we will be able to exist after life here on Earth, we forget that this life on Earth was not the beginning point.

For most of us, eternity stretches in only one direction—forward in time. That leaves us with little concept of, and even less interest in, eternity as history, going back to eons that predate our lives. Without that perspective of eternity, however, it's difficult to grasp an important element of Heaven and life in the hereafter.

God's Heart Toward Us

Heaven is not just about what God has in store for us after this life; it is about what God has been choosing for us from before the foundations of the earth were set.[12] According to Jesus, who said He is going to prepare a place for His followers in Heaven,[13] our spiritual inheritance in the kingdom of God has been prepared "from the foundation of the world."[14] As the Scriptures say,

> Before the mountains were born or you brought forth the earth and the world, from everlasting to everlasting you are God (Psalm 90:2, *NIV*).

In the next chapter we will look at what was going on *in the beginning* when God created the earth and the heavens. *In the beginning* reveals things about *in the end.* But for now, let us focus on God's motivation for making the heavens and earth. That motive clues us in on what He has in store for us.

God loves us. His whole purpose for creating people in the first place can be summed up by the Greek word *agape* (love) that carries with it the notions of "welcome" and "honor." God's agape for us says, "I want to be with you; I want you to be around Me all the time; come, stay with Me forever." He thinks so highly of us and He knows us for who we are individually. Agape thinks well of the ones who are loved. God does not cut short our lives in order to get us back. When the number of days ordained for us is done,[15] He welcomes us home like a father greeting a long-lost child.

The motivation behind a gift is much more significant than the gift itself. Through the years, my wife and I have exchanged many presents as surprises and gestures of love. Few of those gifts survive. Clothes and neckties go out of fashion; earrings get lost; figurines and dishes break; lots of other stuff ends up in garage sales. These gifts are shadows, hints of love. Though our love for each other has none of the material substance of the gifts, the love is more meaningful and more real. The gifts express the reality of the love.

This life is not the only gift God has in store for us. We worry about it coming to an end because we don't understand what is really behind it in the heart of God. There is another gift of life in His heart—a life together with Him, without end.

I purchase most of my best gifts for Pamela when I'm away on a trip. They are expressions of anticipation, ways to say I miss you, statements of "I can't wait to be with you again." God is the same way; this life, at its best, means that in some ways we are not yet completely with Him. That is why we're reminded:

> Return to your rest, O my soul, for the Lord has dealt bountifully with you....Precious in the sight of the Lord is the death of His godly ones (Psalm 116:7,15).

It is important to see this world and life for what they are: easily shaken, easily broken bits of created matter (figurines and neckties) that are utterly insubstantial compared to the unshakable elements of a greater life and world that have existed from long ago.[16] The world as we know it now is like a show on TV. While we're watching the set, our minds automatically block out all the other visual stimuli in the room; we only see the picture on the screen. However, when the show is over, our awareness returns to the greater reality of the room and the whole house. So it will be when this life-show is done: we will return to a greater reality.

In this book we are going to take a look at Heaven and life after death from God's perspective. We will look closely at the few descriptive details highlighted in the Bible, but more than that, we will explore the many marvelous and wonderful truths surrounding Heaven and God's heart for each of us. Not only will we see Heaven in an entirely new light—one that makes the hope of going there all the brighter—but we will also see how

Heaven is woven more tightly than we ever imagined into the tapestry of our current spiritual life.

Notes

1. See Job 1:21.
2. See Judges 4:17-22.
3. See John 20:25-29.
4. William Wordsworth, in reference to his poem "Ode: Intimations of Immortality."
5. Ibid., line 185.
6. See Ecclesiastes 3:11.
7. See Ephesians 3:20.
8. Judges 13:18.
9. See Hebrews 8:5.
10. Hebrews 11:3.
11. See Genesis 1:2.
12. See Ephesians 1:4.
13. See John 14:2.
14. Matthew 25:34.
15. See Psalms 90:12; 139:16.
16. See Hebrews 12:27,28.

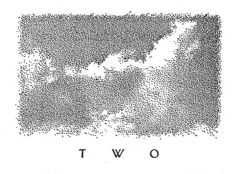

T W O

THE HEAVENS AND THE EARTH

Why did God make the heavens and Earth?

Are stars and comets divinely meaningful?

Do we have "guardian angels"?

Like most people, my grasp of things heavenly was a muddle of many notions swirled together, which is fine for certain ice cream flavors and hearty soups, but not for the place where I was going to spend a very long time! The faint picture I had of Heaven, even as an adult, was both incomplete and composed of mismatched pieces. I certainly cannot claim to have anything close to a complete portrait today, but at least enough is clear to paint some wonderful images. As the Bible says, here on Earth we see only dimly, as if through a darkened glass.[1] But the dim picture at least offers a glimpse of what mysteries and delights await us in Heaven.

With that understanding of certain uncertainty, and an awareness of our limitations as finite beings in grasping the infinite wonders of Heaven, let us begin to construct a picture of what we can know about it.

Every amateur jigsaw-puzzle assembler has had the feeling that the pieces now spread out on the card table do not actually go together. There is no way they can add up to the neat picture on the front of the box. That is how I felt about the many pieces in my "what-Heaven-will-be-like" box. The box didn't even have a clear picture on the front, and I couldn't tell for sure if the pieces I was trying to connect were even right side up.

Without a clear picture to refer to, the only way to construct a jigsaw puzzle is to start with the edges, preferably the corners. That is what we will do in this chapter—start with some corner pieces of Heaven that will later allow us to see a more vivid picture of what it will be like when we get there. As more and more pieces are fitted into their proper places, each additional piece gets easier and quicker to situate. In the beginning, though, doing a jigsaw puzzle takes patience.

Because Heaven is so wonderful, so incredibly different from what we can know and experience on Earth, we will never be able to construct a complete description of our forever home with God before we get there. But that doesn't mean we can't know more than most of us presently know about it. The Bible doesn't tell us everything about Heaven, but it does tell us more things than most people realize.

First of all, the primary focus of the Bible on the subject of eternity is on revealing just how much God loves us and wants to be with us. In fact, when the Bible defines eternal life, it is not in terms of location or duration but in terms of relationship with God:

> This is eternal life, that they may know Thee, the only true God, and Jesus Christ whom Thou hast sent (John 17:3).

The "eternal life" is in His Son. It is so interwoven with His person that "he who does not have the Son of God does not have [eternal] life."[2] This is a very different concept than some people have about an eternal soul—a life essence that will live forever and travel beyond its earthly limitations, regardless of its relationship with Jesus Christ. Eternal life is not an aimless wandering about in the cosmic reaches of the ever after; eternal life is centered on God. He is the source of that life. Eternity is not an empty, endless stretch of time, like a long desert highway heading off wherever people with ideas about how to spend it want to go. Eternal life is a constant unfolding of delights with God, who wants relationship with us forever. That is why He gave the life of His only Son "that whoever believes in Him should not perish, but have eternal life."[3]

IN THE BEGINNING

A Timeless Order

In order to grasp what Heaven will be like, we should start with an understanding of things in the long-ago beginning when God made the heavens and Earth. Looking back at what He made for our beginning (Eden) will give us a good glimpse of what He has made for our ending (Heaven).

The entire heavens and Earth, which God made *in the beginning* of earthly time, are called the cosmos. A fresh look at the cosmos—how it was made and what it is like—will be the beginning corner piece of our jigsaw puzzle. The word "cosmos" comes from the Greek word *kosmos*. Like most conceptual words, it can have several meanings, depending on its context in a sentence, but its most basic meaning is "an arrangement, an adornment, an order."[4] That order is an underlying principle or set of laws that holds the individual pieces of the world together in a sensible whole.

Philosophers like Aristotle sought to define the unifying order of the physical world. One of the most enduring intellectual legacies from Greek philosophy is this notion that the cosmos as a whole is ordered in such a way that it gives purpose and meaning to all of life. According to Aristotle, human reason and observation can and should discover the timeless order, the deeper meaning of temporal, physical things.[5] Hence, both the philosopher and the scientist are looking for the same thing—the one intuitively, the other empirically.

"It Is Good!"

The order in the cosmos God created is not arbitrarily chosen. God's order is a thing of beauty and goodness and life. When a landscape architect lays out the grounds of an estate, he or she can do so according to the alphabetical sequence of the plants' botanical names. But that would miss the whole point of having the garden look its best. What makes a good layout has more to do with the qualities of each tree, shrub and plant, and how they go together. The same is true of clothes outfits: a pale yellow blouse will never go with a red skirt; plaids and stripes are another fashion gaffe.

Whether it is a natural talent or an acquired skill, having an eye for how things ought to be arranged to look their best is an attribute many of us lack. Not everyone has "eyes to see." For instance, decorators can make an otherwise ordinary room look spectacular because they understand which colors go together and which do not. They see in terms of texture, symmetry and accentuating themes. Most of the rest of us say "Uh, nice chair." Asking a person with "the eye" and a person without it to decorate identical rooms, using the same pieces of furniture, the same window treatments (decorators' word for curtains) and the same accessories, will result in a *kosmos* of two very different-looking rooms.

God is the Maker of the cosmos and all of its parts, and He is the One who knew best how to arrange it to declare His majesty and goodness.[6] That is why, upon completing Creation, He exclaimed, "It is good!"[7] When God arranged the worlds, everything was fabulous. Each part of it was arranged and situated for maximum beauty and effect.

AND GOD SPOKE...

In the beginning, God framed the physical world according to His word. He made things the way He wanted them to be. God spoke and called light out of darkness; He brought forth seed-producing plants and trees.[8] He expressed Himself and revealed what was true of His desires for humanity through what He created with His words:

> For since the creation of the world His invisible attributes, His eternal power and divine nature, have been clearly seen, being understood through what has been made (Romans 1:20).

In ancient Near Eastern cultures, words themselves were viewed as more than just symbols (sounds) with meaning. Words also had an inherent power to effect consequences, much like we might view a curse or a blessing. A divine word, especially, was believed to contain creative dynamics that could act upon the physical world.[9] Thus, the word of God is more than just a promise, more than a mere statement. It is a creative, reality-producing force that has acted upon the cosmos from the beginning of time.

In the Old Testament we witness the creative word of God. God spoke and earthly life sprang into being, ordering itself according to His way: "By the word of the Lord the heavens were made,...for He spoke and it [creation] was done."[10] Not only does God's word give order and meaning to life, but it also is the source of all life! This has exciting implications for our study of Heaven, because God's word is eternal; therefore, the pattern that made and sustained things in the beginning will be the same as the pattern in the end. So what was the pattern by which God made the heavens and Earth? According to what blueprint did God make things? It all has to do with His Word.

The Word Template

The spiritual power of the word of God has something of a counterpart in ancient Greek philosophy. The philosopher's term for words with creative ordering power was *logos*. Though it originally meant "word" or "speech," the term "logos" came to embody the "divine reason" that governed humanity and the cosmos. God's Logos was present from the very creation of the world. In the midst of the constant flux of life, the Logos kept things in the universe related to one another on a higher plane.

The New Testament gives us a more detailed picture of the Logos that was in the beginning, when God created the heavens and Earth. The apostle John begins his narration about Jesus Christ with language that draws upon both the secular understanding of the Greek mind and the spiritual sensibility of the Hebrew Scriptures:

> In the beginning was the Word [Logos], and the Word [Logos] was with God, and the Word [Logos] was God. He was in the beginning with God. All things came into being by Him, and apart from Him nothing came into being that has come into being. In Him was life, and the life was the light of men. He was in the world, and the world was made through Him, and the world did not know Him. And the Word [Logos] became flesh, and dwelt among us, and we beheld His glory, glory as of the only begotten from the Father, full of grace and truth (John 1:1-4, 10,14).

The Logos is Jesus Christ. He is not just an unspoken, impersonal principle as in Greek philosophy. He is the whole incarnate Word of God—everything that God wanted to communicate into the cosmos from the beginning. He is God's pattern and entire composition for all creation.

The Master Composer's Love Song

Most of us remember writing compositions in school; almost

none of us knew why those dreaded three-page writing assignments titled "What I Did Last Summer" were called compositions. Writing a composition is the act of putting words and sentences together in accordance with the rules of grammar and rhetoric. Yuck! No wonder we never learned why they were called compositions.

But there are musical and artistic compositions as well—things of wonder, not schoolroom drudgery. The composition of a song we love has all the parts—lyrics, harmony and rhythm—arranged in complementary patterns. Though every part is different, each fits within a larger design. As the Master Composer, God created a cosmos of incredible beauty. All of its pieces—things seen and unseen—have their being and place in His composition. I suspect that is why the angels were shouting and singing when the worlds were made.[11]

In Jesus the fullness of deity dwells.[12] He is everything that God wants to communicate to us on Earth. That is why the Bible says:

> God, after He spoke long ago to the fathers in the prophets in many portions and in many ways, in these last days He has spoken to us in His Son, whom He appointed heir of all things, through whom also He made the world. And He is the radiance of His glory and the exact representation of His nature (Hebrews 1:1-3).

This analogy of Jesus being God's composition is not to suggest that Jesus Himself was created like the universe was created. He was "in the beginning with God."[13] Jesus is like the correct grammar that underlies it all. Using other terms, Jesus is both an active agent in the creation of the cosmos as well as a kind of template for it. He is the firstborn of all creation:

> For by Him all things were created, both in the heavens
> and on Earth, visible and invisible, whether thrones or
> dominions or rulers or authorities—all things have been
> created by Him and for Him (Colossians 1:16).

We cannot get an accurate picture of Heaven if we try to glimpse it outside of its place in the cosmos composed by God. Heaven is a place of our final calling, where we will be with God forever. Unlike here on Earth, things in Heaven will always remain in their intended order. That is why it will be such a great place when we get there.

It also explains why so much of this life has turned out so sadly. Forces and people, who do not have "the eye" that God has, have rearranged and subverted the pattern by which He situated the cosmos. Like careless teenagers we have moved things around; we have taken what God decorated and we have done violence to it. Truly we have messed up the room and not known how to make it right again. That is the essential activity of sin—doing things with or to parts of the cosmos so that their original intent is violated. By going against God's way, sin is always against God Himself.[14] When we commit sin, we are making a statement of rebellion and independence—setting ourselves as the ones who can order the universe our own way.

COSMIC UNCONSCIOUSNESS

During my freshman year at UCLA, I came across a note pinned to one of the many bulletin boards on campus. If you were going to be driving to San Francisco for Christmas break, there was no point in paying for all the gas yourself. Offer a ride and get some gas money from someone you would likely pick up hitchhiking anyway. Some hapless student, who was either desperate or inventive, posted this plea: "Help the cause of Cosmic Consciousness by giving me a ride to S. F." I suspect that student had little interest in cosmology. He was just trying to find a ride guru. But if he really wanted to become conscious of the cosmos, what should he have known?

Where does Heaven fit within the cosmos?

First of all, "cosmology" should not to be confused with "cosmetology." The root word of these two terms is the same, but they are the studies of two vastly different subjects—the complexities of the universe and what constructs make the worlds more understandable, as opposed to the complexions of humans and what compounds make people more beautiful. In modern society, we generally have a better grasp of cosmetology than we do of cosmology.

The Making of the Cosmos

Through the ages, many views of the cosmos have been expounded in Western culture. The ancients believed that the gods surely lived in the heavens because the celestial bodies like the Moon and the Sun affected or controlled such terrestrial phenomena as the tides, the seasons and the dawn. The Greeks added a mathematical and scientific construct to the heavens, reasoning that the movement of the planets was part of the Divine Reason governing the cosmos.

Medieval cosmology, portrayed in Dante's epic poem *The Divine Comedy,* borrowed heavily and in equal parts from Aristotle and Ptolemy. Corresponding to the planetary spheres—from the Sun to Saturn—seven heavens ascended in concentric circular planes from Earth. A seven-tiered purgatory and a three-tiered hell rounded out the spiritual cosmos that Dante believed mirrored the physical cosmos. Satan was in the lowest hell; God reigned in the highest Heaven.

By the early eighteenth century, Heaven and hell were no longer viewed as physical locations, and the starry heavens had been demystified. The Newtonian cosmos was like a machine created by God but then left to run mostly on its own, according to basic physical principles and laws like gravity. To the average person of the day, the universe was mechanical, not spiritual.

Our self-awareness as individual humans is completely at odds with the idea of an oblivious cosmos that will offer up no meaning or intentional arrangement for our existence.

With the advent of the modern scientific era and its high-powered observational instruments, the cosmos became for most people a vast, incomprehensible universe without limits and without meaning. Rather than being created by a knowable, personal God who cares about each person on Earth, the cosmos became distant and aloof. God was left out of the paradigm.

Add an evolutionary twist to the immensity of the cosmos, and people become only one of many species living on only one of many planets in one of many solar systems, swirling through but one of countless galaxies. Our self-awareness as individual humans is completely at odds with the idea of an oblivious cosmos that will offer up no meaning or intentional arrangement for our existence.

A Scientific View of the Cosmos

At the end of the millennium there is an unspoken faith among many people that modern science can see everything there is to see. Telescopes and microscopes are more and more powerful. DNA mapping is almost complete. It won't be long before the physical heavens are mapped, too. This has led to the belief that nothing else exists but what we can see with our instruments. That's why most of us have a schizophrenic view of the cosmos. On the one hand, the cosmos has been shown to be merely physical and mechanical. On the other hand, we cannot give up the sense of eternity in our hearts. The universe is so vast that we think, *Surely there's more "out there" than what we've yet discovered.*

Most of the interest in life on other planets is an attempt to resolve this mental conflict. A universe without any mystery, without any life but on planet Earth, strikes us as utterly impossible. The modernist view of a purely physical cosmos leaves no room for spiritual inhabitants in the heavens. So, at most, people hope to discover alien beings from outer space who travel in some kind of spaceship to reach Earth. Aliens have replaced angels in our scientific cosmos.

The material skepticism and the profound alienation of the postmodern mind-set have made the notion of Heaven almost irrelevant. Many GenXers, for instance, find so little promise reliably offered to them about matters in this life that the prospect of any certainty or hope after this life seems too ridiculous to dwell on. The modern and postmodern paradigm clouds our ability to see Heaven as it is depicted in the Bible. People unconsciously begin their search for Heaven on physical and scientific terms, wondering where a spiritual world can possibly be hiding. After all, we have discovered black holes, supernovas and dwarf stars, not to mention many new galaxies. We have looked on the other side of the Moon, and Heaven is nowhere to be found.

What is the biblical view of the cosmos and how the stars and planets figure in with the Heaven that awaits us after death? What does the Bible say about the heavens?

A Biblical View of the Cosmos

The Hebrew word for Heaven (*shamayim*) is related to a root word meaning "aloft"; its Greek counterpart (*ouranos*) stems from a similar adjective that is best translated "elevated." Both the Hebrew and the Greek words that we commonly translate as "Heaven" refer less to a physical, spatial direction pointing up, and more to a dimension *above and at a different level from* here on Earth. When we speak of the heavens as geographically above us, we are slightly missing the point. It only takes an enterprising fifth grader a short time to figure out that the people in Perth, Australia, are pointing in the opposite direction than the people in Oslo, Norway, when they try to pin a direction to the heavens.

It may surprise you to learn that the Bible speaks of three heavens, not just one! In the beginning, God made the heavens (plural) and Earth. The only actual numbering of the heavens comes in an account when the apostle Paul tells of the time he was "caught up to the *third heaven*."[15] To understand what the Bible says about Heaven, we must begin by grasping the plurality of what we call the heavens. Here are a couple more verses that describe the existence of more than one heaven:

> Behold, to the Lord your God belong heaven and the highest heavens, the earth and all that is in it (Deuteronomy 10:14).

> To Him who rides upon the highest heavens, which are from ancient times; behold, He speaks forth with His voice, a mighty voice (Psalm 68:33).

Of course, our interest is primarily in the Heaven where we're going to spend eternity, but each of the heavens mentioned in the Bible gives us additional understanding about the highest

Heaven where God dwells and where we will live forever.

The fact that there are three heavens has nothing to do with different levels of spiritual enlightenment or attainment, as is the case in some other religions like Hinduism, or the three degrees of glory (the telestial, terrestrial and celestial kingdoms) of Mormonism. The three heavens in the Bible correspond to what we call the sky and outer space, the *first heaven*; the invisible spiritual dimension that surrounds Earth, the *second heaven*; and the *third heaven*—the place where God lives and where believers in Jesus Christ will live for eternity.

THE FIRST HEAVEN

The first heaven in the biblical cosmology—the atmosphere and outer space—is described as a vault above Earth.[16] It is the realm of the clouds, lightning and rain, as well as the intergalactic region of the stars, planets and moons. The first heaven is purely a vast physical composite, though it can inspire many thoughts and feelings.

We know that sunsets come from dust in the atmosphere; windstorms are the result of high- and low-pressure zones, as reported on nightly news programs; pelting hailstones are simply refrigerated raindrops. So why do we feel what we feel when we stare into the night sky? Shooting stars, a full moon enveloped in a misty ring and Venus hanging low in the heavens on a warm summer morning all resonate with something deep inside of us. The physical handiwork of God in the first heaven inspires awe, even in the hearts of people who do not believe in Him.

A large portion of the awe we feel comes from the magnitude of the first heaven; we are also struck with how alien and foreign it is to our dimension of life. The sky and the firmament surrounding

Earth constitute a far different realm from the one in which we live. Atmospheric phenomena like whirlwinds and lightning, as well as extraterrestrial phenomena such as solar flares, black holes or the northern lights, are otherworldly but not unbelievable. Though we can't see the stars during the day, we do not doubt their existence. In the same way, we should not doubt the existence of spiritual realities just because we can't see them all the time. What makes the first heaven—the sky and space—a heaven is not its spiritual qualities but its otherworldly, ethereal ones.

Where Physical and Spiritual Intersect

Though the first heaven is not spiritual in nature, it does interact with and influence things on Earth, and God uses it to instruct us. For instance, God told Abraham to "look toward the heavens, and count the stars,"[17] as a way of explaining how numerous his descendants would be. Earthly navigation is based on reckoning with the stars, and our yearly times and seasons correspond to activity in the first heaven. As a metaphor for truth about how God intersects the affairs of mankind, "the witness in the sky is faithful."[18] It is no accident that God caused a new star to shine in the night sky as a herald of His Son's birth on Earth. That is how God intended things on Earth to work—for us to receive a measure of light, instruction and direction from the first heavens:

> Then God said, "Let there be lights in the expanse of the heavens to separate the day from the night, and let them be for signs, and for seasons, and for days and years; and let them be for lights in the expanse of the heavens to give light on the earth"; and it was so (Genesis 1:14,15).

Our lives are lived on Earth, but we exist partly in the overlap between the sky and the ground, between the first heaven and Earth. Happenings in the first heaven do sometimes have a readout on Earth and are observable in our world. There is some causal relationship between the first heaven and Earth. We are aware of some of the things that go on in the first heaven but not all of them. Jesus used this awareness of another dimension of life to explain matters in the spiritual dimension to Nicodemus. John 3:3 records that Jesus had told Nicodemus that he must be "born again [from above]." To make His point about how things work in the spiritual dimension, Jesus says,

> The wind blows where it wishes and you hear the sound of it, but do not know where it comes from and where it is going; so is everyone who is born of the Spirit. If I told you earthly things and you do not believe, how shall you believe if I tell you heavenly things? And no one has ascended into heaven, but He who descended from heaven, even the Son of Man (John 3:8,12,13).

By explaining how God works in one of the heavens, Jesus drew a parallel lesson for another sphere in the cosmos. Jesus knew how things work in the spiritual realm because He is "from above."[19] He is from Heaven. Near the end of His earthly ministry, Jesus told Pilate the same thing—that "[His] kingdom is not of this world."[20]

What is true of God in the first heaven is also true of Him in the others. In exactly the same way that the Sun's rays warm us or rain drenches us, we should expect the spiritual heaven to penetrate and affect our daily lives, though it is far above Earth. If we adopt Jesus' parallel mode of instruction, we can learn things about Heaven from things in the first two heavens.

The Inhabitants of the First Heaven

Each dimension of the cosmos is inhabited by a different nature of "being." Each heaven has its hosts. The first heaven is populated by the "birds of the air" and the "starry hosts." One of Jesus' best-known teachings centers on the inhabitants of the first heaven. He tells us to consider the "birds of the air [heaven]" and how our "heavenly Father feeds them."[21] His point is that God cares for the inhabitants of one sphere (Earth) in the same way that He cares for those of another (the first heaven). God is the Lord of Hosts—of all the hosts in the heavens and on Earth.

The planets, moons and stars—those galactic bodies that inhabit the unfathomable reaches of the physical cosmos—are both foreign and familiar to us on Earth. The fact that stellar bodies are real and yet so different from anything on the earthly plane we humans inhabit gives them a mysterious quality that some people are inclined to worship. From earliest times, cultures have worshiped the Sun and the Moon and the stars. Mystery religions and astrology have tried to connect the hosts of the physical heavens with events on Earth. People throughout human history have interpreted comets, solar eclipses and other astronomical sensations as signs and portents of things to come—disasters, revolutions, etc. Mark Twain had great fun with such superstition in his novel *A Connecticut Yankee in King Arthur's Court*.

Intuitively, some people feel that the happenings in another, higher cosmic plane must somehow affect our life on Earth. The temptation is to attach spiritual significance to these hosts of the first heaven. But God decries the uselessness and impotence of astrologers, "those who prophesy by the stars, those who predict by the new moons."[22] He says it is an evil deed to worship "the sun or the moon or any of the heavenly host."[23] God warns us not to look to the physical heavens for spiritual answers:

> And beware, lest you lift up your eyes to heaven and see
> the sun and the moon and the stars, all the host of heaven,
> and be drawn away and worship them and serve them,
> those which the LORD your God has allotted to all the
> peoples under the whole heaven (Deuteronomy 4:19).

The hosts of the first heaven, like the first heaven itself, are merely created things. They are not the Creator. They are otherworldly but not spiritually significant to the destiny of humankind. The way that stars, planets or comets may line up or move through the nights has no meaning at all for what happens in our personal, earthly experience.

God "stretch[ed] out the heavens."[24] Our days are in God's hands, not in the paths of the stars. Since His word created and scattered the stars across the vast tapestry of the first heaven, we should never imagine that the way the stars are strewn has any significance to how He wants us to live. Jesus taught us that the best way to live is by "every word that proceeds out of the mouth of God"[25]—not according to the alignment of the starry hosts.

Astral bodies are as physical as birds in the air. As the NASA space program continues to explore our universe, our metaphysical awe of the planets and stars becomes diminished by the pictures and samples of dirt and rocks sent back to Earth. Only when heavenly bodies remain impossible to reach in our existing, physical humanness do they retain their spiritual aura. If we can "get there from here" physically, "there" cannot be the location of the Heaven we are hoping for after we leave this physical life.

If the first heaven is not a spiritual dimension, what does it have to do with the Heaven where we will go when we die?

A Vastness We Cannot Measure

The physical parts of the first heaven—the atmosphere and the firmament—are realms above Earth. Their physical distances and measurements place them at a dimension beyond our world. Their physical proximity to Earth and beyond it is what makes them a heaven—above and beyond the earthly realm. The highest mountain on Earth, Mt. Everest, stretches 29,028 feet into the air. The peak of K2, the second highest point on Earth, is nearly 800 feet lower—but still 5.5 miles up. Our atmosphere stretches 50 miles above Earth, roughly 9 times further than the top of K2; and the Moon, the nearest heavenly body, is 238,857 miles away. Let me do the calculation for you: The Moon is more than 43,430 times higher and further away from sea level than the tip of Everest!

The dimensions of the cosmos are so huge that familiar earthly measurements have little usefulness or meaning. That is why we use the speed of light to measure cosmic distances. A beam of light travels 186,000 miles (seven times around Earth) in one second. Our sun is eight light-minutes above the ground we stand on; the nearest galaxy to our Milky Way is Andromeda—2 million light-years away. Scientists believe there are distant galaxies as far as 10 billion light-years beyond us. The physical distance in the cosmos is meant to communicate a profound spiritual truth to us. It tells us about God:

Is not God in the height of heaven? Look also at the distant stars, how high they are! (Job 22:12).

The proportions are mind-boggling. The yardsticks and odometers that serve us well on Earth are less than trivial once we leave our world. A light-year is too great a measure to apply on Earth. This gives us another truth to grasp about Heaven: Earthly things will seem utterly insignificant there. The highest heights of the earthly realm are dwarfed into nothingness compared to the furthest heights of the first heaven. That is why God says:

For as the heavens are higher than the earth, so are My ways higher than your ways, and My thoughts than your thoughts (Isaiah 55:9).

There is still another truth to grasp from the first heaven about Heaven our eternal home. We acknowledge that we cannot inhabit the physical heavens in our existing bodily condition. We are Earthbound. We cannot breathe in the vacuum of outer space, nor can we travel the incredible distances. Just as our earthly bodies are not suitable for the first heaven, so in parallel fashion they are not suitable for Heaven. That is why Jesus tells us we must be born again (born from above):

That which is born of the flesh is flesh, and that which is born of the Spirit is spirit. Do not marvel that I said to you, "You must be born again" (John 3:6,7).

We will explore the subject of our heavenly bodies in chapter 5, but for now, let us simply acknowledge that "flesh and blood cannot inherit the kingdom of God."[26] We cannot live in Heaven the way we are now living on Earth. We must be changed and further capacitated for a dimension of life that is as far above our present life as the farthest reaches of space are above Earth.

A Handiwork We Cannot Deny

In college I had friends who took art history courses, as a result of which they were able to spot the traits of famous artists in their works. Instead of just seeing a painting with lily pads, these people saw a Monet; instead of a squiggly Sun on canvas, they saw a Van Gogh. Brush strokes, colors, moods and themes set one painter's works apart from all others.

So it is with the heavens. God is the Maker of the heavens and the earth.[27] They communicate God's style; as the Bible puts it in Psalm 19:1:

> The heavens are telling of the glory of God; and their expanse is declaring the work of His hands.

His glory is like His reputation—what people know about Him, what is really true of Him. Seeing the expansive marvels of creation causes us to think about God. That is why when we look across a desert vista at twilight or count falling stars or train a camera at thunderheads piling up in the Sierras, we think

---

When we look across a desert vista at twilight, or count falling stars, or train a camera at thunderheads piling up in the Sierras, we think about God. Without even intending it, we act like art historians and see a Creator, not just a wonder of nature.

---

about God. Without even intending it, we act like art historians and see a Creator, not just a wonder of nature. No one can deny the work of Monet or Van Gogh when trained to spot their artistic distinctives. In the same way, no one can deny the Lord's mark:

> For since the creation of the world His invisible attributes, His eternal power and divine nature, have been clearly seen, being understood through what has been made, so that they are without excuse (Romans 1:20).

THE SECOND HEAVEN

The sky and outer space are physical. All their inhabitants are composed of elements found on the periodic table, that dreaded wall-hanging in high school science class that we were supposed to memorize. Earth and the first heaven share this elemental fact. Though Mt. Kanchenjunga, Earth's third highest peak, and the moons of Jupiter are far apart in the cosmos, they are both made of the same basic stuff.

This is what sets the second heaven apart from the first heaven. They are each made of completely different elements. The second heaven is not tangible or material in earthly terms or senses. It is not composed of the same substances that make up the ground, the air or things in outer space. The elements of the second heaven are spirit in nature.

Every beginning art student knows that if a drawing is going to be true to life, it cannot be sketched in just two dimensions. Artistically, the first two dimensions—height and width—convey much of what can be seen in real life, but depth is what brings full perspective. Life is not two-dimensional, but three. So it is with the heavens. The physical (first) heaven creates a flat rendition. It measures things perpendicularly to one another on a surface plane. Height and width can only create an equation to describe the area of an object, not its volume. Depth is everything beyond what can be physically perceived on the surface. That is the perfect picture of the second heaven.

The second heaven is the invisible, spiritual dimension of reality.

The spirit world, the realm of the second heaven, is every bit (and then some) as real as the world in which we live. It exists in a state all its own, composed of elements more real and more wondrous than what our eyes can see. As surely as the sky is bigger than Earth itself, and as surely as outer space is bigger than our atmosphere, so the reality, the magnitude, the significance of the second heaven supersedes that of the lower first heaven and Earth.

The second heaven becomes easier to conceptualize when I consider just how empty and hollow "solid" things are. The table I put my coffee cup on—indeed, the cup itself—is mostly empty space. The actual physical matter of the atoms that constitute the table and the cup is only a fraction of their size. The rapid movement of the atomic particles makes the table and the cup seem more solid than they are.

As we saw earlier, though people live on Earth, they also live partly in the first heaven, breathing substance from the atmosphere. In like manner, though we live in the physical world, we also have our being partly in the second heaven. When God created humankind, He formed our body out of the dust of the ground, but He breathed into that physical body the breath (spirit) of life.[28]

In the next chapter we will explore the difference between the human soul and spirit, but for now in our discussion, it is at least obvious that our earthly bodies cannot live forever. The life after death we want to know about cannot possibly involve our earthly bodies. God made our bodies to live on the physical plane, and He made our souls to inhabit the higher plane of the second heaven.

A Foot in Both Worlds

According to Paul, we who believe in Jesus Christ have been blessed with spiritual blessings in the heavenly places, where we have already been seated with Him in the presence of God.[29] In Acts 17, Paul's famous sermon on Mars Hill in Athens reminded people that God, who made the world and all things in it, since He is Lord of Heaven and Earth, does not live in physical structures in our dimension. Instead, it is we who "live and move and exist" in a dimension beyond the physical.[30]

Indeed, we are children of God invited to share in His (spiritual) nature:[31]

> Being then the offspring of God, we ought not to think that the Divine Nature is like gold or silver or stone, an image formed by the art and thought of man (Acts 17:29).

We already have the kind of "nature," or constitution, of beings who inhabit the spiritual dimension. Death will separate that "nature" from our physical "nature" (bodies). Knowing that we are already partly inhabiting the second heaven makes the complete transition into it after death somewhat less bewildering. It is normal to fear death in the same way that we worry about going into a dark passage. We do not know what is there, and we worry that we will not be able to see our way. It's like a foggy day when you can't see 50 yards ahead. You worry about getting into the fog until you realize you are already in it. We are already spirit-beings; we do not have to worry about becoming ones.

Inhabitants of the Second Heaven

The invisible realm of the spirit is all around us. Like the physical heaven and the earth, the second heaven has its hosts: a myriad of angels and other beings who are found gathered around God's throne,[32] in "heavenly places"[33] and "roaming about on the earth."[34] Here in the second heaven are found both the legions of God's angels and spirits of evil. The first heaven has birds, planets and constellations, like Orion and Pleiades. In each realm of the cosmos, the "bodies" are made of suitable substances. So it is in the second heaven. The hosts are spiritual ethereal—more akin to breath than bone, more like the scent of perfume than liquid in the bottle.

In 1955, two British climbers got permission from the Sikkim government to scale Mount Kanchenjunga on condition that they would not actually climb all the way to the top—and disturb the gods. There was no need for the precaution. Spiritual beings inhabit the second heaven; they are not tied to surface places on Earth or to the physical heaven above Earth.

The inhabitants of the second heaven probably do not resemble one another any more than the hosts of the physical heaven and Earth do: Mars does not look like Uranus; our moon has very different features than a nebula. Massive sperm whales, who sleep nose down, suspended vertically in the great deeps and who dive hundreds of yards straight down to feed on large squid, bear little likeness to hummingbirds. There is no way to characterize the features of all spirit-beings any more accurately than we might try to describe the features of all colors.

What do the "beasts of the field" look like? How would we describe phenomena in space? What do black holes, dwarf stars and asteroids have in common except the heaven they inhabit? What can we say about all sea dwellers—giant squid, plankton and hermit crabs—except that they partake of the substance of their realm of the cosmos? In the same way, beings in the second heaven are not like bodies on the earth or in space, and neither are they all like one another. Different sorts of creatures roam the deep; different kinds of beings inhabit the second heaven.

Angels

The Bible gives us a fairly extensive list of inhabitants of the spiritual dimension of the cosmos, but it does little to describe them in particular. The purpose of this book is not to detail the forces and entities of the spirit world, nor would it be wise to speculate about their constitution, because the Scriptures do not go into that kind of detail. But a short summary of different kinds of beings in the second heaven is helpful.

From what we can gather in the Bible, the second heaven is mostly populated by angels. Despite all the recent attention given to angels, and some of the dubious claims made about them, we know only a little about them. They are ministering spirits whose presence impacts our dimension of the cosmos like a wind or a flame affects things.[35] Though physically intangible in our world, they can affect our lives and our world.

Angels are God's representatives who deliver revelation and interpretation of spiritual visions, as well as messages, from the spiritual world to people. That is why we call them angels (from the Greek *angelos,* meaning "messenger"). They can call out to people from the second heaven.[36] They sometimes come to people in their dreams, like one did to Jacob[37] or like the angel who warned Joseph to flee to Egypt to protect baby Jesus.[38] When angels do become visible in our dimension, they do so suddenly. For instance, an angel "suddenly stood" before the shepherds to announce the birth of Christ.[39] Angels appear as though out of nowhere. That is because they do not come from some other place on Earth. They come from another realm beyond it. When Gabriel came in to tell Mary about God's plan for her,[40] he did not come through a door from outside of her home; he came through a dimension from outside of her world.

Angels sang and shouted for joy when the worlds were made.[41] The Bible mentions several kinds of angels, from the cherubim who blocked the way to the tree of life[42] and whose form looked both human and animal to Ezekiel in his vision,[43] to the seraphim who have three sets of wings.[44] There is a destroying angel that took the lives of Egypt's firstborn[45] and one who smote Israel because David boasted that his strength was in the number of his subjects, rather than in the Lord.[46]

At times, angels can move physical objects on Earth: an angel "descended from heaven" and rolled back the stone from Jesus' tomb;[47] another angel opened the prison gates that held disciples in Jerusalem and in Antioch.[48]

The Work of Angels

Not everything we hear about angels—from books or movies—is valid. The culturally popular concept of guardian angels is a good example of how people will unintentionally accept a "truth" about Heaven that is not really a picture from the Bible. Though there are many books about guardian angels and a great deal of interest in them, the whole notion of guardian angels comes from only one rather obscure verse in the Bible that records Jesus' words:

> See that you do not despise one of these little ones [children], for I say to you, that their angels in heaven continually behold the face of My Father who is in heaven (Matthew 18:10).

The context for this verse is that Jesus is answering His disciples' question about who will have the highest rank in His coming Kingdom. He tells them that whoever humbles himself and becomes like a little child will become significant in the Kingdom. He urges them to remove the pride in their lives that would make them despise children as being spiritually insignificant. They do not realize that things in the spiritual dimension work very differently from how they work on Earth.

Age and social standing dictate status on Earth among people, but in the heavenlies they do not. Childlike faith and trust are far better than "grown-up" competitiveness and pride. Just as Jesus tells His disciples that the path to spiritual greatness comes through servanthood,[49] He explains that simplicity and lowliness will lead to true significance in the kingdom of God.[50] The point of Jesus' words is that children should not be dismissed as unimportant in the spiritual scheme of things. Their angels have as much access to God as those of any adult!

Whether or not individuals "have their own angels" who have been given special duty by God to protect their charges (in the same way that He commanded His angels concerning Messiah[51]), and what exactly such angels might do, we do not know for certain from the Bible. Nothing else is said about angels as guardians. Angels of God are generally referred to as "ministering spirits, sent out to render service for the sake of those who will inherit salvation,"[52] but that does not necessarily imply personal valet-type service or divine guidance for people who have no relationship with God.

In fact, the term "guardian" is not found in the Bible with reference to angels. One of its few uses is in reference to Lucifer, whose name was changed to Satan when he was driven in disgrace from the presence of God because of his rebellion:

You were anointed as a guardian cherub, for so I ordained you. You were on the holy mount of God; you walked among the fiery stones. You were blameless in your ways from the day you were created till wickedness was found in you. Through your widespread trade you were filled with violence, and you sinned. So I drove you in disgrace from the mount of God, and I expelled you, O guardian cherub, from among the fiery stones. Your heart became proud on account of your beauty, and you corrupted your wisdom because of your splendor. So I threw you to the earth; I made a spectacle of you before kings (Ezekiel 28:14-17, *NIV*).

We are warned not to let other people's visions or "the worship of angels" defraud us of our true prize in Jesus Christ.[53] In fact, Satan's messengers can disguise themselves as "good" angels because the devil "disguises himself as an angel of light."[54] Many of the stories and teachings of supposed guardian angels are in direct opposition to the teachings of the Bible. Because God would never contradict Himself, we must conclude that any spirit-being who brings another teaching than that of the Bible cannot be of God. Paul puts it this way:

> But even though we, or an angel from heaven, should preach to you a gospel contrary to that which we have preached to you, let him be accursed (Galatians 1:8).

The other use of "guardian" in reference to someone is about Jesus, who is called the "Shepherd and Guardian" of our souls.[55] He is the only one who has paid the price to forgive us and redeem us from the power of death. He alone preserves and protects us, because "there is no other name under heaven that has been given among men, by which we must be saved."[56] As Peter says of Jesus:

> He is the one whom God exalted to His right hand as a Prince and a Savior, to grant repentance to Israel, and forgiveness of sins (Acts 5:31).

Jesus is a far better Guardian than any angel could ever be. The "angels of God worship Him."[57]

Other Spirit-Beings

There seems to be some sense of hierarchy among spirit-beings of the second heaven. Archangels, like Michael, have greater power in the second heaven than other angels. We see evidence of this in the help given to an angel when he was being hindered in bringing a message to Daniel.[58] This episode reinforces another vital fact about the hosts of the second heaven: They are not all aligned with the purposes of God. The realm of the second heaven is a dimension of both good and evil. The angel from the Lord was being opposed by another supernatural being—the prince of Persia—one of an order of evil entities that hold some sort of sway over nations of the earth.

Just because something is supernatural does not mean it is good. Demonic powers and evil spirits exert their influence on the affairs of mankind. They inspire false religious ideas,[59] and they afflict people with inner torments. Not all the impressions and voices people hear in their minds and hearts come from the Lord. In fact, when people are eager to get in touch with the spiritual dimension, one of the greatest traps they fall into is confusion: They presume that anything from the second heaven must be good because it is spiritual.

Time and again, the Bible warns us to "test the spirits" to be sure they are aligned with the purposes of God.[60] Not every spiritual experience should be believed. Just as God warns us not to consult the hosts of the first heaven for our life's direction, so He admonishes us not to look to the hosts of the second heaven. Astrology is evil, but so too is any effort to contact beings in the spirit world by means of "mediums or spiritists."[61] The point is that not every one of the hosts in the second heaven is from God.

There is little to be gained by trying to figure out the exact workings of evil spirits who inhabit the spiritual dimension of the cosmos, but we do know that they are of different sorts—rulers (arch-princes), powers (jurisdictions), dominions or forces (shaping influences), thrones (seats of authority), etc. The Bible passages that list these evil spirit-beings focus not on the their distinctions but on three facts about all of such wicked forces in the cosmos:

- they are created beings who are no more impressive in their world than we are in ours;[62]
- they are far below and completely subject to Jesus Christ;[63]
- we can, and should, resist their influence.[64]

THE THIRD HEAVEN

If the first heaven is the physical stretch of sky and space and the second heaven encompasses the spiritual dimension, what is left for the third heaven? In the simplest of terms, the third heaven is God's dwelling place. It is where He is. Of course, God is omnipresent—everywhere at once; so to speak of the place where He is can be a bit confusing. It helps to remember that spatial terms and positional descriptions have very little meaning when it comes to spiritual realities. It is like trying to describe colors in terms of pitch or tone or attempting to equate a spot on our planet with a compass direction. Though Alaska is north of California, it is not what north is; neither is Alaska north to those who live there.

In order to relate Himself to us in terms we can grasp, God speaks of the place of His habitation,[65] where He somehow "dwells" in more particular fashion than elsewhere in the cosmos. Though He does "fill the heavens and the earth,"[66] His throne and His temple are "located" in a particular locality within the entire reaches of the heavens:[67]

The LORD has established His throne in the heavens; and His sovereignty rules over all (Psalm 103:19).

That specific locality is where Jesus is seated at His right hand.[68] Though God "is over all and through all and in all,"[69] and though His presence is essentially everywhere,[70] He does not "dwell" everywhere—not on Earth or in buildings made with human hands:[71]

> However, the Most High does not dwell in houses made by human hands; as the prophet says: "Heaven is My throne, and earth is the footstool of My feet; what kind of house will you build for Me?" says the Lord; "Or what place is there for My repose? Was it not My hand which made all these things?" (Acts 7:48-50).

God's sovereignty rules over all the realms of the cosmos—not just Earth, the skies and the vast expanse of the starry host, but also over the second heaven. And yet, not all the hosts in the spirit world are like God's angels who are

> Mighty in strength, who perform His word, obeying the voice of His word! Bless the LORD, all you His hosts, you who serve Him, doing His will (Psalm 103:20,21).

There are parts of the second heaven that exist in a current state of rebellion against the way of God. When Satan was cast to the earth because of his pride and sin, he continued to exist in the spiritual dimension; he did not become flesh and blood, even though he was driven from heaven, "cast...from the mountain of God."[72] At some point in the distant past, a great battle was fought between the angels of God and the devil, with his foul minions. Listen to how the Bible describes what happened then in the spiritual dimension:

And there was war in heaven, Michael and his angels waging war with the dragon. And the dragon and his angels waged war, and they were not strong enough, and there was no longer a place found for them in heaven. And the great dragon was thrown down, the serpent of old who is called the devil and Satan, who deceives the whole world; he was thrown down to the earth, and his angels were thrown down with him (Revelation 12:7-9).

Eventually, the devil became the ruler of the kingdoms of man, and he is called "the prince of the power of the air, of the spirit that is now working in the sons of disobedience."[73] The devil is a spirit inhabiting the realm of the second heaven, but banished from the third heaven where only those spirit-beings who obey God have access. As we will see later, the second heaven can be thought of as the entire spirit realm of the cosmos.

The third heaven constitutes the vast majority of the second heaven. But in and around this tiny speck in the cosmos called Earth, there are what we might call regions where evil spirits and powers have a temporary measure of authority to exert their own wills against God.[74]

God cannot abide the presence of unrighteousness, so He is not side by side with demonic beings; "God is light, and in Him there is no darkness at all."[75] Just as on Earth there is the need to welcome the kingdom and the will of God,[76] so also does the need exist for the will of God to be brought into parts of the spirit world we call the second heaven.

The first heaven is comprised solely of physical substance and inhabited exclusively by natural beings; the second heaven is populated only by spirit-beings; of those spirit-beings in the second heaven, only the ones that are fully aligned with God Himself reside in the third heaven.

A Focused View of Heaven

Part of what makes our image of Heaven and life after death so fuzzy is the way people unintentionally blur the three heavens into one and the mistake they make of thinking that Heaven is centered around the earth. For instance, the popular notion that after death we will sit on clouds (in Heaven) is a result of mistaking the *for now* physical heaven with the *forever* spiritual Heaven. Realizing that there are three heavens that exist around us now will help us get a more accurate picture of the Heaven where we will spend eternity with God.

Most of us have a concept of Heaven that confuses details, mixes biblical images and misses much of the wonder. If we want to learn what Heaven will be like, we have to sort out the details and correct the misconceptions. It would be easy for someone like me to miss the whole point of the grandeur of Heaven if I only think about strumming a harp forever. I consider harp playing from an earthly perspective—lots of practice, sore fingertips, endless rehearsals. The thought doesn't thrill me because I'm not good at music here on Earth. Only upon reflection do I realize that in Heaven my heart and hands will be able to spontaneously compose melodies of adoration to the Lord more beautiful than any songs ever heard on Earth. That is a dream come true; that is Heaven.

Before we get to the place called Heaven, there is still a lot to learn about the other heavens and Earth. Until we understand the second heaven and how it affects Earth, we cannot fathom the full dimensions of our eternal home.

Notes

1. See 1 Corinthians 13:12.
2. 1 John 5:12.
3. John 3:16.
4. Colin Brown, ed., *The New International Dictionary of New Testament Theology*, vol. I (Grand Rapids: Zondervan Publishing Company, 1971), pp. 521-26.
5. Richard Tarnas, *The Passion of the Western Mind* (New York: Ballantine, 1991), pp. 69, 70.
6. See Psalms 19:1; 97:6.
7. See Genesis 1:31.
8. See Genesis 1.
9. Colin Brown, ed., *The New International Dictionary of New Testament Theology*, vol. III (Grand Rapids: Zondervan, 1971), pp. 1081-1117.
10. Psalm 33:6-9.
11. See Job 38:7.
12. See Colossians 1:19.
13. John 1:2.
14. See Psalm 51:4.
15. 2 Corinthians 12:2, italics added.
16. See Job 22:14.
17. Genesis 15:5.
18. Psalm 89:37.
19. John 8:23.
20. John 18:36.
21. Matthew 6:26.
22. Isaiah 47:13.
23. Deuteronomy 17:3.
24. Isaiah 44:24.
25. Matthew 4:4.
26. 1 Corinthians 15:50.
27. See Psalm 89:11.
28. See Genesis 2:7.
29. See Ephesians 1:3; 2:6.
30. Acts 17:28.
31. See 2 Peter 1:4.
32. See 1 Kings 22:19.
33. Ephesians 6:12.
34. Job 1:7.
35. See Hebrews 1:7.
36. See Genesis 22:11.
37. See Genesis 31:11.
38. See Matthew 2:13.

39. Luke 2:9.
40. See Luke 1:28.
41. See Job 38:7.
42. See Genesis 3:24.
43. See Ezekiel 1.
44. See Isaiah 6:2.
45. See Exodus 12:23.
46. See 2 Samuel 24:15-17.
47. Matthew 28:2.
48. See Acts 5:19; 12:3-11.
49. See Matthew 23:11.
50. See 1 Corinthians 1:26-31.
51. See Psalm 91:11; Matthew 4:6.
52. Hebrews 1:14.
53. Colossians 2:18.
54. 2 Corinthians 11:14.
55. 1 Peter 2:25.
56. Acts 4:12.
57. Hebrews 1:4-6.
58. See Daniel 10:12-21.
59. See 1 Timothy 4:1.
60. See 1 John 4:1.
61. Leviticus 19:31; 2 Kings 21:6.
62. See Colossians 1:16.
63. See Ephesians 1:20-23.
64. See Ephesians 6:10-12.
65. See 1 Kings 8:30,39.
66. Jeremiah 23:24.
67. See Psalm 11:4.
68. See Ephesians 1:20,21.
69. Ephesians 4:6.
70. See Psalm 139:7,8.
71. See Ecclesiastes 5:2; Isaiah 66:1.
72. Ezekiel 28:16.
73. Ephesians 2:2.
74. See Ephesians 6:12.
75. 1 John 1:5.
76. See Matthew 6:10.

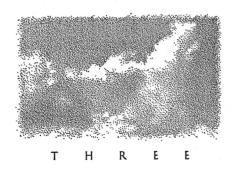

T H R E E

Natural and Supernatural

How is our daily life affected by the supernatural?

Can we look into the heavens from Earth?

What is the difference between our soul and our spirit?

Catching a faint scent of my wife's perfume that lingers on the shoulder harness of the seatbelt is my favorite thing about driving our car. Some mornings neighbors probably wonder what I'm doing with my face pressed against the strap on my shoulder, but it's worth it to me to draw breath deeply and be reminded of her. That is similar to how the things of the *second heaven* are intangibly part of the physical world we inhabit.

What has been said so far is that God is the Maker of all the heavens and the earth, what we call the cosmos. The *first heaven*—the atmosphere and (outer) space—as well as the earth itself are physical dimensions in the cosmos. Just as one volume of a set of encyclopedia resembles the others, even though it has very different contents, so in the same way each dimension of the total cosmos bears similarities to the others. And these similarities offer us intriguing details about Heaven.

We cannot grasp what Heaven will be like without understanding the natural *and* the supernatural here on Earth—the realm of spirit and the realm of flesh, the tangible and the intangible, the material and immaterial, what we can perceive with our physical senses and what comes to us more intuitively, or through the "spirit of man." The second heaven touches and infuses all of the cosmos, coexisting with the earth and with the first heaven. Like a spiritual atmosphere, it is side by side with the physical realm in much the same way that the "world" of scents and fragrances rests within and next to the "world" of sights or sounds. The dimensions of the cosmos overlap.

In the physical world, we accept the existence of things like the wind, even though we cannot actually see it. What we see is not the wind itself but the effect that the wind has as it moves about. When the leaves on a tree begin to rustle, we know it's windy outside. That is how the supernatural often shows up in the natural realm. Not often can the supernatural be seen in and of itself. Mostly, we see its effects in the physical dimension of the cosmos. Like my wife's perfume, it presses into the physical world in barely discernible ways.

Many people struggle with questions about Heaven because they are not used to thinking in terms of the supernatural in their daily life. They do not put the natural and the supernatural together on the same cosmic plane until they ponder life after death. The realm of the supernatural is all around us, all the time, and our natural world is affected by it.

Possessing little familiarity with just how normal and real the realm of the supernatural is in our daily existence, most people have a hard time grasping that there is already a great deal of (second) heaven on Earth. I do not mean that Heaven is "where you can find it" in the joys and pleasures of this life. Nor do I mean that Heaven is just a state of mind—a happy, contented feeling of satisfaction with this life.

Such notions about Heaven are very popular and they form the basis of many people's philosophy of life and death. For them, this life is all there is. Since they believe there is no life after death, no such places as Heaven or hell, they turn the place-names into adjectives to describe experiences and times on Earth. When they say something was "Heaven on earth," they merely mean "It doesn't get any better than this." The words "It was hell" simply translate as "It was the worst situation possible." Such misuse of the terms blurs the language of eternity. And it subtly influences how we think about Heaven.

HEAVEN ON EARTH

When I say there is already a great deal of (second) heaven on Earth, I am referring to the fact that the invisible spiritual world interacts with our visible physical world all the time. We just are not aware of it. Our senses are not trained to discern the supernatural.[1] Sometimes in the summer months, I "pick up" the fact that a neighbor is cooking steaks on a barbecue. I know what they are doing because I smell it, not because I hear it or see it. Likewise, I adjust the temperature of the shower each morning, not on the basis of smell or sound but on the basis of feel. Without any one of my senses, I would miss many things in this life, but it would not negate their existence.

Physical reality is made up of things that are perceivable to us and things that are not. There are pitches on the sound spectrum that human ears cannot hear. Parts of our bodies cannot feel physical sensations because they have no nerve endings. We spend a third of our life sleeping—a physical state in which we have little consciousness of the world around us. If even physical reality is sometimes beyond what we can lay hold of with our five natural senses, we should not disbelieve in the supernatural just because we can't touch it or see it all the time.

The hosts of the first heaven affect Earth's seasons and tides. Activity in the second heaven causes more than just a stir on Earth. The second-heaven hosts determine far more than just the turning of the leaves or the pull of the sea; they can affect the turning of lives and the very tides of human history.

When it's daytime, we do not see many of the stars. We may see the faint outline of the moon, but we don't see the stars until it gets dark. Even then, with the natural eye, we only see little pinpricks of light. We have no concept of the magnitude of those stars as suns in their own right. In the same way, only magnified many times over, the natural eye cannot perceive the things that exist in the realm of the spirit. The astronauts and cosmonauts who have traveled into space see the stars all the time. Daytime and nighttime are all the same to them.

Unfortunately, the cultural and intellectual paradigm of the modern world has convinced many people that there is no such thing as the supernatural—or if it exists it only comes into play after one leaves this life. Even those of us who believe in God and who hope to spend eternity with Him in Heaven succumb to the subtle influence of the philosophy of science that tells us not to look for anything supernatural in this life. Heaven and Earth get separated as though different creators made them and as though they have nothing to do with one another.

FAULTY REASONING

The scientific way of thinking has been greatly influenced by rationalism and empiricism—two philosophical perspectives that do not accept any connection between the natural and the supernatural. The empiricists say that we can only know things through our senses and physical experience; the rationalists believe ultimate truth comes purely from thought. That is why most people today put their trust in logic and science. Science and logic tell us that the cosmos is governed by natural laws and is explainable in purely physical or rational (mathematical) terms.

Science tends to study human behavior exclusively in natural terms; it accepts invisible causes and influences only when such variables have an empirical explanation. When scientific researchers come across something in the natural world they can't explain, they use a subtle phrase to keep all discussion and curiosity confined within their paradigm of a two-dimensional cosmos. They say, "Scientists do not yet know what causes...." The implication is that the cause will eventually be found in the natural realm. It never occurs to them that they might be looking in the wrong dimension with the wrong instruments. Their cosmos consists of only Earth and the first heaven.

Most of us do not realize how influenced we are by this way of thinking. In our hearts we know there is more to life than just the physical. But we don't know how to integrate the obvious reality of life after death when we leave this earth with the life we are living on it now. We are partly "Heaven-blind" because the worldview our culture has adopted has made it hard to *see* supernatural colors.

Heaven Blindness

A few weeks ago I went for an eye exam, and by the time I left the doctor's office, I was faced with a cruel choice—bifocals with a line or without a line! Aside from that harsh reality, I was intrigued by the test for color blindness given to me by one of the assistants.

The test is not one you can study for. It is just a series of colored circles about the size of a saucer plate. Inside the circles are various sizes of dots of different colors, and some of the dots form the discernible pattern of a numeral. If your color perception is fine, you can make out the "hidden" number from the colored background. I passed that part of my eye exam. I had "eyes to see." One in 10 men do not. For purely physical reasons, some people cannot see what is so plain to the sight of others.

A color-blind person cannot see the numerals in the saucer circles. Just because he or she can't see the numbers doesn't mean the numbers aren't there. When it comes to the supernatural, things in the second heaven, most people are "spirit-blind." They have a hard time seeing what is there.

That is why Jesus often asked people, "Having eyes, do you not see?"[2]

Leaping Leptons

It is difficult to "see" something we know nothing about. With the rapid increase of knowledge in the world today, I sometimes feel like a foreigner experiencing culture shock; it's weird to realize that much of what I learned in high school no longer applies to the world because of things researchers and scientists have discovered since then.

A good example of how knowledge keeps growing beyond what I learned a couple of decades ago comes from a branch of science called particle physics. This field of science studies really, really tiny things like the atom that most of us remember from our school days. The atom (named for the Greek word meaning "indivisible") used to be called the smallest building block of the universe. Since the days I was in school, scientists have found even smaller particles than the protons, neutrons and electrons that comprise an atom. These tiny bits of matter are called quarks and leptons.

Scientists acknowledge that something keeps breaking down this tangible world to the smallest element, the lowest order. It sounds remarkably like what the Bible teaches us about the spiritual power of sin.

Quarks and leptons, the physical cosmos's smallest known particles, actually come in three sizes: small, medium and large (sounds more like men's clothing). Physicists have discovered an amazing fact that they do not quite know how to explain. Even though the large- and the medium-size quarks and leptons do, in fact, exist in the physical world, their existence is so short-lived that they are always "have-beens" whose stay on the stage of life is almost too brief to count. Apparently, the higher level large- and medium-size quarks and leptons instantly break down into the small-size variety. The physical, tangible world that we see around us is composed only of the tiniest quarks and leptons. It is as though the world we call real is in a process of disintegration and erosion.

I am not saying that the second heaven is made of big quarks and that is why we can't see it. The subatomic particles are merely physical realities that offer us a parallel to understand spiritual realities. Without any spiritual understanding at all, scientists acknowledge that something keeps breaking this tangible world down to the smallest element, the lowest order. It sounds remarkably like what the Bible teaches us about the spiritual power of sin that came into the world and caused the things that God meant to exist to degenerate.

This microdeterioration of atom parts is an aspect of the macrodegeneration of universe parts called entropy—the "wear-out and breakdown" factor in the physical cosmos. Entropy is why I need new glasses every few years. Because of entropy, disorder and degeneration increase over time as the available amount of energy that got things started diminishes. In normal language that means the universe and everything in it is like a new car after you've driven it off the lot! It's downhill from there. Pieces of the kids' partially sucked hard candy will get lost between the seats; dents will appear on the body with increasing frequency after the first one shows up and the engine has begun its countdown to the end.

BEYOND TIME AND DISTANCE

Using the teaching pattern that Jesus employed to draw parallels between dimensions of the cosmos, we learn something more about the second heaven, the realm of the supernatural: Things that can be seen there can be seen only dimly from Earth. When we go from one dimension of the cosmos into another we can see things we could not see that well from where we were. When we get to Heaven we will see and know things that were imperceptible to us on Earth. It's mind-boggling to think of the vastness of the physical heavens and all the phenomena about which we know virtually nothing.

Our natural curiosity bids us to speculate about what might be "out there." We are intrigued by the "Star Trek" mentality; we love to learn about, explore and experience new things—especially in other realms of the cosmos. In Heaven we will come to know more than we could even imagine here on Earth. That is why we are told:

> For we know in part, and we prophesy in part; but when the perfect comes, the partial will be done away. When I was a child, I used to speak as a child, think as a child, reason as a child; when I became a man, I did away with childish things. For now we see in a mirror dimly, but then face to face; now I know in part, but then I shall know fully (1 Corinthians 13:9-12).

The apostle Paul is speaking about the inheritance reserved for us in Heaven that is "imperishable and undefiled."[3] Heaven will not only manifest the glory of God but also His permanence. By believing in Jesus Christ, according to the Word of God, we obtain the salvation of our souls. That is the message of the gospel announced by the Holy Spirit sent from Heaven, by various messengers through the ages. God has communicated His plan for our salvation, but that is just the beginning of what He has in store for us. He will answer every question we still have, once we get to Heaven, with a complete unfolding of all the mysteries, all the hidden things that have been beyond our understanding. His Truth will answer all.

Knowing What to Look For

The Bible acknowledges that spiritual realities are but faint objects we see dimly in a mirror—just like through a telescope. The Hubble space telescope, deployed into orbit in 1990, is looking for specific things with its powerful lenses and cameras. Its mission is to investigate the physical characteristics of celestial bodies, including the formations of stars and galaxies, and to study the evolution of the universe. The European Space Agency's Faint Object Camera on board the Hubble recently sent back pictures of the never-before-seen surface of Pluto. How aptly named that camera is: Faint Object. It sees cosmic phenomena that are light years beyond Earth.

But because it is only looking for distant physical objects, it will not see the place called Heaven. Because it confines its search to the surface dimensions of the first heaven, it will not be able to tell us about what lies even further beyond—the second heaven and Heaven our eternal home. That is the problem most of us have. We do not know how to look beneath the surface or beyond the natural. We do not even know what to look for.

And God knows that about us. He knows that we are incapable of seeing into the second heaven on our own. As surely as the unaided eye cannot see most of what exists in the physical heaven, so most of what exists in the spiritual heavens is beyond our human power to observe. One of Jesus' very first teachings on Earth was that unless someone was born again of the Spirit, he or she would not be able to "see" into the spirit realm.[4] Unless we are touched and transformed by God, our blindness persists.[5]

Taking the Cover Off

How would empiricists learn anything about a place to which they have never been? How would rationalists come to know about a realm that lies beyond what they can think? And for the rest of us who-knows-what-our-philosophy-is-or-if-we-even-have-one people, how are we to learn things about the spiritual heavens?

We need revelations of things that are normally hidden from our sight. The base word for "revelation" in the New Testament is *klepto*, and it can be translated as "cover taken off." People who have a compulsion to steal are called kleptomaniacs. They steal things *under cover*. The word "revelation," if we were to anglicize the Greek, would be "*un*-kleptoed"—uncovered and brought out into the open where it can be seen.

In a sense, there are two kinds of revelation, two ways in which people on Earth can learn about the supernatural dimension: They can be moved into that realm, or things from that realm can be brought to light in this world. By far, the most frequent way in which revelation comes is by things of the spiritual realm of the cosmos coming into the earth, not by people from the earth going into the spiritual dimension.

One of the most humorous examples in the Old Testament of people seeing into the spiritual dimension is the story of Elisha and his servant who faced the Aramean army.[6] The king of Aram and his soldiers were trying to capture Elisha in a city called Dothan. They surrounded the city and cut off any chance for escape. This unnerved Elisha's servant. Elisha, on the other hand, was a prophet and was accustomed to seeing into the second heaven. He prayed that the servant's eyes might be opened to have a revelation of the multitudes of spirit-being angelic soldiers surrounding the besieging army of Aram.

That changed the whole picture, as it usually does when we get a glimpse of what lies beyond the natural. When the soldiers and chariots of Aram launched their attack on Dothan, Elisha prayed almost the same prayer as before, only in reverse. He prayed that God would blind the earthly sight of the Arameans like He had opened the spiritual vision of his servant. God did.

Because He is the Lord of all the dimensions of the cosmos, He can give or take away sight in any of them.

Seeing into Heaven

The New Testament also gives us some examples of people who entered the realm of the supernatural and saw things that could not be seen from Earth. Such an experience happened to the disciples on the Mount of Transfiguration when they beheld Jesus, whose "face shone like the sun," in discussion with Moses and Elijah.[7]

The apostle John also glimpsed things in the spirit realm while he was physically on an island called Patmos (35 miles off the southwest coast of Turkey). He wrote the things he saw "in the Spirit" in the book of Revelation.[8] The sights and sounds he recorded were fantastical and otherworldly. But they were real. Likewise, Stephen, the table-waiter turned evangelist who was stoned to death because of his belief in Jesus as the Messiah, saw "the heavens opened up and the Son of Man standing at the right hand of God."[9]

Perhaps the best known episode of someone seeing into the spiritual realm is that of the apostle Paul, who tells of his "translation" this way:

> I know a man in Christ who fourteen years ago—whether in the body I do not know, or out of the body I do not know, God knows—such a man was caught up to the third heaven (2 Corinthians 12:2).

Paul was not talking about being captured by aliens. He was not talking about grabbing hold of the tail of a comet and being spun out far enough into physical space so that he encountered this other realm. Neither was he referring to some kind of astral projection, or out-of-body experience. Paul was talking about suddenly being able to see into a distant dimension of the cosmos as though someone had given him a spiritual telescope. He was able to glimpse things that were real, but their reality was incomprehensible. He heard things spoken in that dimension that could not be translated in earthly terms; they were too incredible.

In the same way that we should make sure we are not following false teachings that come to us or to others from angels or other spirit-beings, so another caution is in order when we discuss times in the Bible when people were "caught up" into heavenly dimensions. It is no accident that most occult and New Age religions include practices designed to transport people out of the limitations of the physical plane. Nowhere in the Bible do we find an example of someone trying to convey themselves into the heavens. God always initiated such translation and revelation. It did not happen through elaborate rituals, incantations, meditations or hypnotism. Furthermore, all revelation must align with the revealed word of God found in the Bible. Every idea and thought that comes to us out of Heaven must be obedient to the Truth in Jesus Christ:

> For though we walk in the flesh, we do not war according to the flesh, for the weapons of our warfare are not of the flesh, but divinely powerful for the destruction of fortresses. We are destroying speculations and every lofty thing raised up against the knowledge of God, and we are taking every thought captive to the obedience of Christ (2 Corinthians 10:3-5).

Heaven-Sent Revelation

God sent His commandments and spoke to the prophets from Heaven. Peter and others received visions from that realm. As we already know, Jesus came to Earth "from above." He calls Himself "the true bread" that "comes down out of Heaven, and gives life to the world."[10] God sent Him into our world and gave Him a message for us about life the way it was meant to be lived. God wants us to believe His words and to believe that He sent Him. Listen to Jesus' prayer to God, His Father:

> For the words which Thou gavest Me I have given to them; and they received them, and truly understood that I came forth from Thee, and they believed that Thou didst send Me (John 17:8).

He came into this world to tell us about another world. The great hope that we have about the place called Heaven comes from one of Jesus' most famous statements: "I go to prepare a place for you."[11] As surely as He came from the *third heaven,* the abode of God, and returned to it, so will He return to Earth one day:

> And as they were gazing intently into the sky while He was departing, behold, two men in white clothing stood beside them; and they also said, "Men of Galilee, why do you stand looking into the sky? This Jesus, who has been taken up from you into heaven, will come in just the same way as you have watched Him go into heaven" (Acts 1:10,11).

The return of Christ to this earthly plane is closely tied in with other details about our life after death. What happened to Him when He died? Where did He go after He died? These are questions that will help us understand what awaits us after death. We will explore these questions in chapter 5.

At this point in the development of the Heaven jigsaw puzzle, the important fact to note is that the One who promises life after death came into our world as a revelation from God. Throughout His earthly life, Jesus received continual revelation from God as to what He should do and say. He was constantly and completely in touch with and a part of the spiritual dimension:

> Jesus therefore answered and was saying to them, "Truly, truly, I say to you, the Son can do nothing of Himself, unless it is something He sees the Father doing; for whatever the Father does, these things the Son also does in like manner" (John 5:19).

More so than anyone else who ever lived on Earth, Jesus dwelt within the natural and supernatural spheres of the heavens and Earth. He grew in wisdom and stature before God and man;[12] He is the Son of God and the Son of Man—fully human like us, yet fully God. On several occasions people heard God speaking with a voice coming out of the heavens, declaring that Jesus was His Son. The proclamation God made through a star in the first heaven, and through an angel in the second heaven, He made Himself out of the third heaven.

Jesus told Nicodemus that he had to be born again; flesh cannot function in the realm of the spirit. But neither can spirit fully function optimally in the physical dimension. That is one reason why the Holy Spirit "came upon" Mary. Though Jesus pre-existed His life on Earth in a "form of God," He had to take upon Himself the likeness of earthly flesh in order to share fully in the things of our world.[13] If He had not been fully human, He could not have tasted death; if He had not been fully God, He could not have come back from earthly death.

The natural things of Earth will grow increasingly faint

when we see more of the supernatural things of God. The more we realize that the spirit dimension coexists with the physical dimension, the more comfort we will find in our transition from a mostly physical, natural existence to a spiritual life in *Heaven*. That transition brings up the discussion of two terms that tend to be used interchangeably by most people, but they must be distinguished before we can grasp what awaits us after this life. Those words are "soul" and "spirit."

WHAT MAKES US DIFFERENT

When stars die, they may have a moment of glory (if those of us on Earth see them "fall"), but the cosmic realm in which they end up is the same as that in which they began. They live out their lives and die their deaths all in the first heaven. The meteors that hit Earth's atmosphere are never more than physical objects, without life after death. Stars have no power to reach into the realm of mankind to shape lives or destinies, and they have no power at their death to transcend the physical limits of the first heaven.

Likewise, when a sparrow falls from the sky, its life is over forever. It has no kind of life inside of it other than the natural life that enabled it to function in its dimension of the cosmos. When the question comes up about whether or not Millie the hamster (or Sputnik the dog) will go to Heaven, it probably is not the right time to delineate the different definitions of "soul" and "spirit" as they are used in the Bible. As we will see, their meanings offer little hope for hamsters but incredible promise for humans after death.

Little boys and girls who have just lost a pet do not need to know that hamsters and geese and crocodiles all lack souls. Though animals live on the same earthly plane as humans do, they are not alive on the inside as conscious, personal beings. Animals have no sense of personhood or self; they do not dream of the future or regret the past; they do not reason, emote or battle with their conscience. Neither parrots nor stars, neither Sputnik nor Millie will ever be anything more than physical bodies. They are born only of the substance fitting for the physical world.

Not so with people.

The Soul Animates the Body

When God formed Adam out of the physical, earthly substance that was appropriate to humankind's place in the cosmos—making us out of dust, the same stuff that our world is made of—God also breathed into Adam's being the substance appropriate to our other place in the cosmos—the realm of the second heaven. Our earthly frame is made of clay; our heavenly essence is not.[14] The cells of sheep may be cloned, but the essence of our souls can never be.

People have a place in the cosmic order that places them on a different level from that of sea dwellers and water buffalo. Though we are created beings like the birds of the air and the lilies of the field, we are different from all others because, of all the hosts in the physical dimensions of the cosmos, only people have souls. We are not just flesh and blood.

We have consciousness and feelings, moods and longings. We can anticipate a cheeseburger as well as digest it. We are aware of things that have no tangible existence: funny feelings, subtle atmospheres and unexplainable confidences. We love. We question. We feel nostalgia or nausea over years gone by. Our will chooses a course; our conscience comments on that course. These are not activities and attributes of clay alone.

The word "soul" in both Hebrew (nepes) and Greek (psyche) is related to the act of breathing. But more significantly, it refers to a somewhat abstract concept that might be called the "inner life" of a human being—the personality and vitality that moves a person to follow the course he or she follows in life, in the same way that breathing appears to animate the physical body. A body that is not breathing is generally not moving.

The soul has the power of will, reason and emotion; and it reveals its life in the choices we make, the thoughts we think, the desires we have, the vices and virtues we possess. What we are conscious of when we are conscious of ourselves is our soul. It is our personality, the sum of our inner drives and understandings and memories. It is who and what we are as individuals, distinct from other people in what we feel, know and choose. To use an old expression, the soul is the "seat" of our whole being—life as we uniquely live it out and experience it.

Animals do not have souls. Neither do they have spirits.

The Spirit Moves Us Beyond the Natural

As with the word "soul," the Hebrew (*ruach*) and Greek (*pneuma*) words for "spirit" are connected with the idea of "air," or "breath." But the emphasis of "spirit" is not on the air itself or on what that breath moves, as is the case with "soul." Rather, spirit is best understood as what moves the soul. Spirit is air set in motion, breath that has been animated. Think of it this way: Air is the least tangible physical substance in our earthly realm of the cosmos. It is part of the first heaven, part of the overlap of that dimension with our own.

The ancient Greeks and the Hebrew patriarchs observed that sometimes something turned the still air into wind. That something they named spirit—a substance that we have learned is part of the second heaven.

Jesus used the analogy of the wind to teach Nicodemus. Just as the air is moved by a force that cannot be seen, so are people who are born of the Spirit. The soul is the inner life of people, comprised of awarenesses and activities and sensations that put us in touch with and enable us to participate in qualities and proportions of life that are completely unknown to animals. Hamsters know nothing of contemplation, singing or falling in love. They have no language or capacity for such soulish activities that make up most of the life we live as humans. In like manner, the spirit is another sort of inner life that is supposed to connect us with a kind and quality of life beyond the natural.

In less symbolic language, *spirit* is what connects man to the spiritual realm, the realm of reality beyond ordinary physical

---

Souls are natural; spirits are supernatural. Many of the misleading and unbiblical notions of life after death blur the distinction between soul and spirit.

---

perception and power. Just as an animal knows nothing of soulish sensitivities, so the human soul knows next to nothing of spirit-sensibilities. Beasts are not soul-sentient; they have no awareness of their inner feelings. And neither are souls spirit-sentient; they are mostly insensible to the things of the spiritual dimension of the cosmos. Each person has a soul and a spirit. The physical bodies of people will expire like those of all animals,[15] but the soul and spirit within us will not.

Bodies are physical; souls are natural; spirits are supernatural. Many of the misleading and unbiblical notions of life after death blur the distinction between soul and spirit. We will see why shortly, but first let us look at a few passages from Scripture that contrast the human soul and spirit. Perhaps the most telling of such scriptures speaks about the power of the Word of God to delve into the innermost reaches of our being to discern what is really going on:

> For the word of God is living and active and sharper than any two-edged sword, and piercing as far as the division of soul and spirit, of both joints and marrow, and able to judge the thoughts and intentions of the heart (Hebrews 4:12).

Likewise, we see the distinction when Paul prays blessing for his friends in Thessalonica:

> Now may the God of peace Himself sanctify you entirely; and may your spirit and soul and body be preserved complete, without blame at the coming of our Lord Jesus Christ (1 Thessalonians 5:23).

Alive in the Spirit

Adam is called "a living soul" in contrast to Christ, who "became a life-giving Spirit."[16] Furthermore, we are told that a "natural man" (i.e., one who only functions at a soulish [psyche] level) cannot understand the "things of the Spirit of God" because they only make sense to someone who appraises them at a spirit (pneuma) level.[17] When God reveals things to us, He primarily does so by His Spirit to our spirit.[18] Our souls, though eternal in the sense that they (we) will never cease to exist, are not tuned to the frequency of God. They are like an AM radio; they pick up lots of stations, but they can't get any FM signal. The human soul is meant to be the directing power for our natural life, not our spiritual life. Just because our soul is functioning doesn't mean our spirit is working properly. That was Jesus' point to Nicodemus: If you haven't been made alive in your spirit, then you cannot see the things of the Spirit of God.

The body, soul and spirit function in different modes of being. Though they overlap like the dimensions in the cosmos, they remain distinct. My body exists in the earthly realm of the cosmos, but it cannot function in that realm without my soul animating it. In the same way, my soul exists in the spiritual realm of the second heaven, but it cannot function in the third heaven without my spirit quickening it.

The Best and Brightest Fall Short

Thoughts and sensations that originate from the human soul—no matter how religious or supernatural they seem—are not necessarily to be trusted. A common thread of falsehood running through philosophy and religion is the notion that the human soul is intrinsically divine, able to reconnect with its immortal beginnings by transcending earthly limitations through discipline, knowledge, meditation or some other means. By confusing soul with spirit, many people have been led astray from their need to be spiritually reborn by the Spirit of God.

Such confusion, though, is very satisfying to human pride that would like to think that nothing is impossible for the "enlightened soul." Philosophies and religions often appeal to the false notion of people's innate goodness or intrinsic divinity, promising freedom from all sorts of encumbrances.

On Earth, and in the first heaven, the human soul with its thoughts, determinations and emotional drives will continue to be capable of extraordinary accomplishments and discoveries. Thanks to human ingenuity, courage and curiosity, our world is developing its collective know-how at a staggering pace. The human soul has been hard at work. But at the same time our world has grown increasingly alienated from the God who made it. Left to our own souls' counsel and guidance, we have gone astray and "sought out many devices."[19] Technological advances do not necessarily lead to moral or spiritual progress. And we should not forget that the soul, with all its sensibilities and powers, cannot keep its earthly tent from folding after several score of years.

This is one of the main traps of humanism. It fails to note that just because people have been capable of wonderful accomplishments on Earth and in the first heaven due to the exertion of the mind and will, it doesn't mean they can do all things. Man is the measure of things only within his own sphere of the cosmos. Nothing we humans can do on our own will enable us to push beyond the cosmological limits of Earth, the sky and space, into the second heaven. No matter how well bred or accomplished or intelligent people may be, they are still of the earth until they become "born again [from above]."[20] Only "that which is born of the Spirit is spirit."[21] As John the Baptist said of Jesus:

> He who comes from above is above all, he who is of the earth is from the earth and speaks of the earth. He who comes from heaven is above all (John 3:31).

"God is spirit," Jesus told the woman at the well.[22] Anyone who wants to approach Him in worship must do so in truth and in spirit, the same mode of God's existence. Jesus kept pointing to the spirit dimension and the impossibility of people accessing it on their own, no matter how sincere or religious they might be. He said to the Pharisees,

> "I go away, and you shall seek Me, and shall die in your sin; where I am going, you cannot come." Therefore the Jews were saying, "Surely He will not kill Himself, will He, since He says, 'Where I am going, you cannot come'?" And He was saying to them, "You are from

below, I am from above; you are of this world, I am not
of this world. I said therefore to you, that you shall die in
your sins; for unless you believe that I am He, you shall
die in your sins" (John 8:21-24).

How interesting that Jesus told some people that they could
not go where He was going, yet to other people He promised that
He was going to prepare a place for them to be with Him forever. As we will see, the difference between the two groups of people ties in with the conditions of their spirits. The good news is
that each of us already has a spirit as well as a soul. We were
made for eternity; we were made to relate to and live in more
than just the physical dimension of reality. Thus, our existing
state (body, soul and spirit) gives great promise for our future
state after death.

And now we get closer to the particular subject of this book.
What happens to us after we die? What exactly did Jesus mean
about dying in our sins? What becomes of our soul and spirit
when our body dies? The next chapter will look at what it means
for us to die and what dying means for us.

Notes
1. See Hebrews 5:14.
2. Mark 8:18.
3. 1 Peter 1:4.
4. See John 3:3.
5. See 2 Corinthians 4:4.
6. See 2 Kings 6:8-23.
7. Matthew 17:1ff.
8. Revelation 1:10.
9. Acts 7:56.
10. John 6:32,33.
11. John 14:2.

12. See Luke 2:52.
13. Philippians 2:6.
14. See Genesis 2:7.
15. See Ecclesiastes 3:19.
16. 1 Corinthians 15:45.
17. 1 Corinthians 2:14.
18. See Romans 8:16; 1 Corinthians 2:11,12.
19. Ecclesiastes 7:29.
20. John 3:3.
21. John 3:6.
22. John 4:24.

F O U R

DEATH: ONE FOE REMAINING

Why do we have flowers at a funeral?

Why do people die; why does God allow death?

Is death a state of oblivion, or are we conscious after death?

On Earth, in the dimension of the cosmos for which our bodily frame is suited, we generally feel resourceful. Until several overpowering disappointments come our way, we enter young adulthood believing we can take whatever life throws at us. If unexpected things come up, we feel like we can handle them and challenge life to take the first swing. On Earth, we've got life by the tail.

Not so underground or underwater. Most people do not like the underground. Even coal miners or diamond diggers, who spend hours deep beneath the earth's surface, do not really like it. Caving enthusiasts (called spelunkers) find excitement in exploring caverns, but if you take away the items they bring with them from the world above—especially light—their fascination quickly turns to a desperate quest to survive. We were not made to live down there.

We associate the depths underground with death. We know that Heaven is up above, so we intuitively conclude that the other place is down below. We do not want to go there—and the depths of this world in the ground or in the sea are too close for comfort. The prospect of death taking us into the ground is psychologically unsettling.

The reason the depths of the earth unnerve us slightly is that they are realms of God's created order that were never meant to have dominion over us. It feels wrong to be at their mercy. In the beginning, when God made the heavens and the earth, He gave humankind stewardship over all the physical realms of the earth and their living hosts.[1] The expectation of death taking us into the underworld violates everything we intuitively understand about our intended place in the cosmos.

In Western cultures, bodies of the dead are usually buried underground (dust to dust) or their ashes are scattered over the sea. Even if we do not read the Bible that closely, we have seen enough movies to know that burials at sea usually include a reference to giving up its dead.[2] No wonder we're ambivalent toward the depths of the sea and of the earth. We don't know what to expect down there; we just know that we were not designed to live in those realms.

THE DITCH AND THE CAVE

The handful of underground experiences in my life have been a mixed bag. Each of my subterranean trips was filled partly with a sense of adventure—going someplace mysterious or forbidden—and partly with terror (as the reasons why the places were forbidden became clearer to me). Two forbidden gateways to the underground world were conveniently located near the house where I grew up in Southern California, just north of L. A., in a town called Saugus. It was a mostly rural area, only recently invaded by vast housing developments.

One of the portals to the underworld was down the hill near the elementary school, about a hundred yards from where Sputnik, my dog, got run over. I don't know if there was any cosmic connection between the place of Sputnik's death and one of my greatest childhood temptations, but right there next to San Francisquito Canyon Road, a storm drain that collected water from the rain (or broken sprinklers that ran all night) emptied out into a ditch.

Some unknown older boys had bent back the locked metal grate that was supposed to cover the four-foot concrete pipe opening in the ditch. Almost no self-respecting eight-year-old boy could refuse an invitation like that. The ditch was open and muddy-wet all the time. The elaborate maze of makeshift bridges (logs and planks) and stepping-stones (any old rock that was big enough to be hard to lift) that the neighborhood guys had constructed was not always enough to ensure uninhibited access to the pipe. Sometimes a foot hit the muck. And stuck.

That is what happened to me the day I swore off going through that portal ever again. I'm not sure what the scientific explanation is for it, but when a boy's tennis-shoe-clad foot steps into Saugus mud, it doesn't slip back out very easily. In fact, it doesn't come out at all unless the boy leaves a sacrifice to the muck gods—his shoe.

It happened so quickly that I still can't recall all the details, but when my foot took an awkward turn and plunged into the muck, I wished with all my heart that I had heeded my parents' instruction not to go near this place. I escaped with my life, but not with my shoe. I learned the hard way that the underworld takes parts of you away.

The other access to dark places in my early life was up the hill near the place we called The Cliff. The face of The Cliff was scary enough, and only the bravest kid in the neighborhood, Donny Perciville, dared to edge across it. Behind The Cliff, three caves beckoned us kids toward adventure. The closest of the three, a man-made cave, had been dug during the gold-rush days. It was not very interesting, just a shaft going into the mountain. The other two caves had more passages and twists, and they went down.

One day I got some firecrackers and tried to initiate a cave-in by setting them off inside the cave. I was smart enough to stand outside and toss the lighted firecrackers into the cave. Nothing happened to the cave. It offered up nothing of intrigue to match my anticipation of an "otherworldly" experience. My one taste of the extraordinary came when I picked up a dud fire-cracker, only to have it flare up in my hand. The underground world burned me.

As sobering as my early encounters with the underworld were, they did not compare with a later episode when I visited a place underground called Moaning Caverns. I discovered that stalactites and other mineral formations under the earth can be exquisite and awe-inspiring when lighted properly. But I also learned that a carefully guided tour of our national caverns is not the same as being all by yourself, lost without light in the midst of stalagmites, deep pools and towering drop-offs. Part of the tour at Moaning Caverns includes a sudden lights-out at the bottom of a huge chamber that has a ceiling which is hundreds of feet back up the staircase the guests have just climbed down.

The blackness is completely disorienting. When the tour guide tells people to put their hands in front of their faces, everyone expects to be able to see something of their hands—a faint outline, detectable movement, at least something! To see nothing, to be completely cut off from all traces of light, causes an instant panic.

To add to the profound shock of the underground experience, the guests are told the story of the cave and how it was originally discovered. Its fairly small opening above the ground belied the treacherous reaches beneath the surface. Apparently, people (who never got a chance to tell anyone about their discovery) had come upon the cave over and over again through the centuries. By dropping to what appeared to be just a few yards down—to the floor of the cave—the would-be spelunkers ended up hitting a steeply angled and very slippery limestone ledge that dropped off without warning or mercy to the very place where the visitors were now standing in total darkness.

"Imagine," the guide said, "what it must have been like to fall into dark nothingness, to hit the ground with such force that your legs were broken, and then to crawl aimlessly about trying to find a way out—when there is no way out!" In this century, when the cave was carefully explored, several skeletons were found of people who had fallen prey to the underworld.

That did it for me. No more caves.

When Flesh and Spirit Part

The eternity that God has set in our hearts, as well as the inevitable passing of friends, family, ourselves—these urge us to learn more about the life of spirit as opposed to the fleeting life of flesh. So, let us confront death and dying for what they are in the light of spirit.

What happens the moment a loved one or someone very close to us dies? The instant it happens, or the moment we hear of it, what grips our hearts? What do we think? What do we know? We have feelings of disbelief and dismay. We remember the last time we saw the person or something we just heard him say a few days ago. Probably our first thought is a struggle to reconcile the details of the last time we spoke to this person with the fact that we will not talk to him or her anymore. Everything inside us cries out, "No, it can't be...it can't be!" Almost always we confront death with disbelief.

But we have another awareness, too. In the midst of all the sadness and fear and regret we feel when a friend or relative dies, we know something very profound. It is more than just a feeling, more than a wishing-upon-a-star-trying-to-make-ourselves-feel-better hope. What we instinctively know is as obvious as someone turning on a light in the room. We feel it in the same way we have felt the sun suddenly warm us when it breaks through the clouds on an otherwise dismal, overcast day. It is especially obvious if we've been in the room with the person who just died.

What most of us discover at such times is a great truth about death: It is not the end. Our friend is not erased, he's just moved;

the one we love has not passed out of existence, just out of contact. It is true we're no longer able to touch them, but they have not dissipated into nothingness. They have not ceased to exist; they have just left the room. All our sensibilities tell us they are still around, even though they're no longer as they have been.

The body they leave behind loses its familiarity so quickly that we know the abandoned flesh is not the true essence of the one we love. It was an "earthly tent" that held them;[3] it was not they themselves. It is made of clay. It feels empty, vacant, used. It is like fine dinner china that looks so exquisitely arranged for the big Thanksgiving meal. The cranberry dish sets off the neatly heaped potato platter. The glasses sparkle; the silver gleams; the leafy centerpiece warms the table. How different the dishes look after dinner, sitting on the counter to await their turn in the dishwasher. The dinner was here, in this house, at this table, on these dishes, but the dishes no longer have that look of life.

Because we live in two dimensions of the cosmos at the same time, inhabiting both the world of flesh and the world of spirit, dying in one of the dimensions does not mean death in the other. We were made in God's image, not just in our earthly attributes and characteristics, but even more so in our spiritual constitution.[4] We are an image (literally a shadow) of God in that we have a spiritual nature, an inner life beyond and above our physical life. This is comprised of all the invisible, intangible aspects of our being, like our personality, our thoughts and feelings, our conscience and our will, as well as those sensibilities that are meant to function in the realm of the second heaven.

For years I had to carry out a nightly ritual of parenthood—carrying water to the kids in the middle of the night. I could fill a reservoir with all the water I carried from the kitchen in little plastic cups to their bedrooms. I don't have to do that anymore. The kids get up on their own, go to the kitchen, fill the (same)

cups and then leave them empty on the kitchen counter. I find
the empty cups every morning, and I wonder which child was up.

Empty cups tell a story. They used to hold something, and
what they held is now somewhere else. It is only gone from the
cup. Now it is in a container far grander, far more wonderful
than colored plastic. That is what the Bible says about believers
when they die. They do not stop existing; they just get carried in
a better vessel—a vessel more suited to the spiritual heavens:

> We look not at the things which are seen, but at the
> things which are not seen; for the things which are seen
> are temporal, but the things which are not seen are
> eternal. For we know that if the earthly tent which is
> our house is torn down, we have a building from God, a
> house not made with hands, eternal in the heavens
> (2 Corinthians 4:18—5:1).

Removing the Training Wheels

Our bodies are like training wheels. Little kids have many misconceptions about training wheels, but only before those wheels
have been taken off their bikes. Graduating to a two-wheeler
from a trike is one of the most significant passages in a child's
life. All seems right in the world when the big day comes and the
training wheels are affixed to the bicycle. Within a day or two the
kid has forgotten all about the trainers—riding around without
a care—until mom or dad suggests taking them off. Then panic
grips the child's soul. "No training wheels? I can't ride without
training wheels!" But we know they can. They will learn to balance without the wheels and end up not even missing them.

In the same way, we will do far better than we fear we will do
without our earthly bodies. The natural body is comprised of
clay,[5] and it is feeble. It betrays us with its inherent vulnerabilities

and weaknesses. Gravity and bacteria subject it to indignities, and without calories and sleep, fatigue is unavoidable. It grows restless during long stretches of time, and its aches or stomach pangs are enough to keep us distracted from the real issues of life. It tires more easily as the years pass, and it grows more and more independent of our wishes. We do our best to take care of it, but it still grows stiff, leathery and frail.

Such a base body would never do in Heaven. Ours is a body that bears the likeness and image of Earth's imprint. As surely as we have had a body that worked here on Earth, just as fish with their different constitutions work under water, so, too, will we have a body that has been designed to work in the realm of spirit.[6] Each realm of the cosmos has different kinds of bodies; all physical bodies are not alike—stars are not like birds; fish are not like mammals; people are not like any other creature.[7] So it is that our human, Earth-dimension body is not like our human, Heaven-dimension body.

Death in One Form, Life in Another

The Bible says our physical body will undergo a transformation:

> It is sown a natural body, it is raised a spiritual body. If there is a natural body, there is also a spiritual body (1 Corinthians 15:44).

That is why flowers are such an integral part of memorial services in our Western culture. Flower bulbs are rather homely. So are seeds. But they have a hidden life contained within their bland exterior. We plant bulbs and seeds in faith, believing that they will turn into flowers. The bulbs themselves were not intended to grace tables in a vase. They do not do anything to brighten the landscape of a yard if they are simply tied to a trellis or laid in rows on the ground's surface next to a walkway.

We want them for their other, more beautiful bodies. We plant them in expectation that they will give rise to stems and flowers. One body flourishes underground; the other is more suited for above ground. A daffodil and gladiola each have two bodies—one for below, one for above.

A Darryl and a Gladys are made in the same fashion. The vibrant flowers at a funeral remind everyone that we have two lives, lived in two dimensions: flesh and spirit. One body works on Earth; the other body is more suitable for Heaven. As the Bible says, "If there is a natural body, there is also a spiritual body" whose splendor far outshines that of our earthly body.[8]

The hood above the stove in our kitchen has the usual light and fan designed to make cooking easier and less invasive (we do not want the smell of certain items spread throughout the house). Both the fan and the light have two settings: high and low. At our house we keep the light on low at night, so none of us stumbles over anything if we get up for water or a snack. Because we use the low light most of the time, it has burned out more often than the higher setting. In fact, we've never had to replace the two-way bulb because the brighter light burned out. The same casing holds two filaments—one for the high light and one for the low. They work independently of one another. One can burn out without affecting the other.

So it is with us as living beings. We have two filaments—one that functions dimly on the physical plane and one that burns brightly in the realm of spirit. Physical death simply means that our earthly filament has broken. Nothing has been done to our essential element in the heavenlies. When we die, we do not pass into oblivion or nonexistence. We simply leave our earthly casing and pass completely into the spirit realm of the cosmos. Our physical bodies may go into the ground or into the depths of the sea, but our inner self does not go with them.

The instant we die, we separate from our bodies like stages of a rocket. What once held us and enabled us to move on Earth no longer has any connection with us. We will not be living in there any longer. If you've ever gone back to visit a former home and discovered that it has been demolished, you understand the lack of connection between your body and your soul/spirit. Because a former dwelling was torn down after you moved out, you are not now left homeless.

What happens to our bodies when we die has nothing to do with what happens to our soul and spirit. That was Jesus' point when He encouraged His followers to fear God, not man.[9] Though people can do us bodily harm, they cannot do anything to affect the destiny of our soul and spirit. Our body and our soul/spirit have different futures.

We are not just creatures of the earth; we are also creations of the heavenlies. The fact that we have life in two dimensions of the cosmos makes us different from stars and water buffaloes and ears of corn. The milk of dairy cows can be transformed into cheese, and the flesh of their cousins can be turned into top sirloin when they die, but there is no life in cows other than that which animated them in the pasture and allowed them to chew the cud. Freshwater trout and Maine lobsters get caught and eaten. Nothing is left of them except bones and shell. They have no more soul or spirit than an ear of corn that is picked and shucked and turned to husk. They are dead and no longer exist on Earth. They never did exist in the realm of spirit.

Our physical life eventually breaks. No matter how vigorous our exercise, no matter how determined our diet, we age. Nothing can stop the inevitable wearing down and out. That is why the preacher in the book of Ecclesiastes cries, "Vanity of vanities; all is vanity!" He is not trying to be depressing—saying there is no point to anything in life because we all die anyway. Rather, he is advising everyone that they should think in terms of life beyond the earth and above the sun. Our flesh and our spirit are destined for different endings: dust to dust; spirit to spirit. When we die, our two lives separate from one another and pass completely into their respective dimensions of the cosmos—one remaining with the clay and the other ascending into the heavens:

> For man goes to his eternal home while mourners go about in the street. Remember Him before the silver cord is broken and the golden bowl is crushed, the pitcher by the well is shattered and the wheel at the cistern is crushed; then the dust will return to the earth as it was, and the spirit will return to God who gave it (Ecclesiastes 12:5-7).

Facing the Inevitable

Most people are afraid of dying—not just of the possible suffering leading up to death or the separation from loved ones—but of dying itself. That fear of death enslaves us in a desperate life struggle.[10] It begets one of the most primary of all human motivations: self-preservation. Almost nothing takes precedence over our desire to stay alive. Even in the midst of incredible pain or utter brokenness, we want to keep from dying. In the cases of people who take their own lives, their goal is actually to keep from dying, over and over again, from their incredible pain or sorrow. In a backward kind of logic, they believe that anything is preferable to continually dying the way they are dying.

To stop the suffering, they end their lives. They cast themselves into the unknown, gambling that nothing could be worse in the hereafter than what they are experiencing now. Their fear of the unknown is overcome with the greater dread of the known—the hopeless pain of mind or body that they live with daily. Concluding that any end is preferable to simply carrying on with such agony of body, mind or heart, they find justification for doing the unthinkable—taking their own lives. I suspect that for most people, however, the uncertainty of what will happen after death makes them fear death itself.

Death is a final sentence, a verdict without appeal. It has the last word on our life on Earth. It is sad, gruesome, usually untimely, bitter and offensive. It stands out in stark contrast to the quiet hand-holding of a couple celebrating their silver anniversary, of a ponytailed eight-year-old girl playing dress-up in her room, of an eager student on his first day at the university, of a young boy trying in vain to keep his voice from cracking when he says hello to friends at the mall. Death is so opposite, so contrary, so hostile to life.

Why Do We Have to Die?

If God is the Maker of all the heavens and the earth, if He created life, then where did death come from? How could something so utterly different from His intentions for and arrangements of the cosmos ever find its way into the way things are? Could it be that our revulsion toward death is a clue from our soul/spirit that death is not part of how things were meant to be? Death is foreign to us. It is a stranger with whom we cannot get comfortable no matter how many times we're introduced. Death doesn't fit. It was not part of God's original order.

The fundamental wrongness of death is our first clue to its origin. "Wrong" has many definitions. For instance, "wrong" can mean not in accord with an established arrangement (coming at the wrong time); inappropriateness (saying the wrong thing); not working properly (something wrong with my hearing). When something is wrong, it is amiss—out of place, out of sync. All of these meanings for "wrong" can be summed up in the Greek word *hamartano*—"to miss the mark" (as in an archery contest).

Poor aim sends an arrow off mark—which leads to the loss of the archery contest. The English verb for *hamartano* is "to sin."

Hamartano is any wrong that creates an unintended loss, problem or disadvantage. When we forget to check our calendar and we miss a crucial business luncheon; or when we miss the "formal attire" comment on the dinner party invitation and show up to a gala event in a sports coat and jeans—only to be stared at by the other guests in their tuxedoes and evening dresses—we have "sinned." The *miss*-take itself, as well as the resulting situation we find ourselves in, are both parts of *hamartano*.

The point of God making the heavens and the earth could not be just to have it all end, to have you and me simply cease to exist.

When we go against God's arrangements and His instructions for how to live life, we *hamartano*. That wrongness takes us away from the destination God had in mind for us. It is like not following a set of directions for how to get to a dinner party to which we have been invited. We make a series of wrong turns and get lost. Missing the correct turns means missing the celebration. We end up in the wrong place. That is where death comes from. As the Bible puts it, "The wages of sin [*hamartano*] is death."[11]

Death is the "wrong place," the opposite of what God intends for us. That is why our soul/spirit recoils from it. Deep within us we know we were not made for that end. The point of God making the heavens and the earth could not have been just to have it all end, to have you and me simply cease to exist. Life was the goal; it was the mark and the prize all in one. By choosing our own course instead of God's, we choose the way that leads to death.[12]

Death entered the realm of mankind when the first person elected not to follow God's instructions for how to live.[13] Adam and Eve were fooled into believing that God was trying to deny them something that would make life better for them than what He had already arranged. They believed that their lot in life would be vastly enhanced if only they could get hold of what God told them not to touch.

They disregarded the boundaries of God's order, and that violation allowed sin to flood our race. As a result of their wrong turn, all of humanity was set off course—to live in a cosmos of chaos and death. "The sting of death is sin [*hamartano*]."[14] Death (life other than how God arranged it) was our choice, so death (life away from God) became the only kind of life we knew.

The Deeper Meaning of Death

So how does this relate to Heaven? Does death's origin hold some understanding for us about life after death? It does. But in order to see the connection between where death itself came from and where we will go after we die, we must redefine death in terms that are not just physical.

As we have seen, our modern mind-set views life empirically. Physical facts predominate. So when most people think about death, they do so in language that ends up hiding some wonderful prospects for life after death. Life is more than breath and brain waves. Death is much more than the absence of breath and brain waves, although that is how most people in our culture would define it.

Death has a deeper meaning. There are two basic components of death: first, people who die end up missing the rest of life. They are cut off from their would-have-been future on Earth with all its sights, sounds and events. Second, when someone dies, he or she loses contact with the loved ones "left behind."

When people die, they cease to be able to interact with those who live in the realm they have just left.

Here is the crucial point: Regardless of the realm of the cosmos in which death occurs, it always means two things—individuals who die are cut off (1) from the life they would have had and (2) from relationship with those who loved them in that dimension.

That is the meaning of death. Its implications are far more significant than its descriptions. The physical reasons why someone on Earth will no longer be with us are nothing compared to the actual fact that they will no longer be with us. Death takes people away from the future they would have had. Although this seems so obvious, it has huge implications for our condition on Earth right now and for what will happen to us when we die.

We Must Be Born Again

As we've been learning, we exist on two planes of reality at the same time. Our bodies inhabit Earth; our spirits inhabit the second heaven; and our souls overlap both worlds. What we haven't explored fully is the condition of the spirit's existence in the heavenlies. According to the Bible, a person can be dead in spirit but alive in body and soul. In fact, that is the condition of anyone who has not received forgiveness for his or her sins.[15] Though we came into the physical dimension of the cosmos and have lived our lives here, we were long ago stung by the spiritual *hamartano* committed by Adam and Eve. In the realm of spirit, the second heaven, we were dead—cut off from the life God planned for us and removed from God Himself because of our trespasses and sins:[16]

> Therefore, just as through one man sin entered into the world, and death through sin, and so death spread to all men, because all sinned (Romans 5:12).

That spiritual death had two consequences—the same out-comes death always has: First, we were taken away from the spiritual life we were meant to have. Second, we were cut off from relationship with God, who loves us. It is not at all facetious to say that death makes things turn out very differently than intend-ed. It changes everything. In the state of death, we perpetually experience the exact opposite of God's intentions for us.

Most families have experienced a vacation when nothing turned out as intended. Maybe it was a trip to Hawaii during the wettest week in recent history, so everybody had to stay inside the (cheap) hotel room with no view of the ocean. The rental car was an open jeep, and Mom twisted her ankle trying to catch one of the kids who was falling off the planter box he had been told several times to get off. To make matters even worse, the wife's brother's family was only supposed to share that hotel room one night, but a foul-up with the reservations turned it into five nights! Instead of a life full of good, bounty, joy and under-standing, death is an existence of trauma and disappointment.

When sin caused our spiritual death, we did not cease to exist. Far worse, we lost out on a dimension of life in the spiritual realm and on the ability to have relationship with God. Adam and Eve were excluded from the life they could have had in Eden. Their sin caused them to hide "themselves from the presence of the Lord God among the trees of the garden,"[17] and it cut us off from relationship with Him in the second heaven.[18] As we will see, the whole point of Jesus coming into our earthly realm of the cosmos was to enable us to pass out of our spiritual state of death and back into the condition of life.[19]

The good news for us in our study of Heaven and life after death is that death in one realm of the cosmos does not neces-sarily affect life in another. As surely as we have been able to live on Earth even while being dead in the spiritual dimension, so will we live on in the spiritual dimension after our death in the physical world. You and I have already been dead once, spiritually speaking; in fact, we were stillborn in spirit at the time of our physical birth. That is why Jesus said we have to be born again. God grants the gift of spirit life to all people who accept forgiveness for their sins through Jesus Christ.[20] God "raises the dead and gives them life."[21]

When we were still dead in our sins, we did not notice any impairment in our natural life. And we cannot tell much difference between someone who is alive in Christ and someone who is not—at least in their ability to think and move in this life. Having a dead spirit does not mean that people stop being alive on the earth. In exactly the same way, having a dead body does not mean we will stop being alive in the second heaven.

Restored Relationship with God

The ultimate consequence of sin is death, and since all of humanity has sinned, the devil temporarily holds sway over parts of the second heaven that are in rebellion against God.[22] Satan, himself, was cast down from the presence of God, but through his deceitfulness toward Adam and Eve He has obtained authority over the very beings that God intended to rule the earth. That is why he could legitimately offer dominion over "all the kingdoms of the world, and their glory" to Jesus during the wilderness temptation.[23] The devil is "the prince of the power of the air" who sets the disobedient "course of this world."[24]

Too quickly, and inaccurately, our culture translates eternal life as simply living forever (as opposed to dying). Eternal life is not just a life that goes on without end. It is a quality of life that directly corresponds with all that has been in God's heart for us since the beginning of the cosmos. It is life with nothing missing and nothing wrong. It is life without fear, pain, disappointment or shame. There will be no pride or envy, no hate or confusion, no regret or disorder.

Eternal life is life without death—not death as the ending point, not death as the final curtain, but death as any state of being or condition of life that is different from God's intentions. Since God's original intent for us is to have fellowship with Him, the greatest outcome of "death" is absolute loss of relationship with the Lord. And the greatest outcome of eternal life will be restored relationship with God in the heavens:

> And this is eternal life, that they may know Thee, the only true God, and Jesus Christ whom Thou hast sent (John 17:3).

As surely as Christ has been raised from the dead and seated at God's right hand "in the heavenly places,"[25] so too have we been "raised up with Him, and seated with Him in the heavenly places."[26] Though we are not conscious of that spirit life in the second heaven, we who believe in Jesus are already living in eternity! The final passage of our conscious awareness into that realm will not be frightful or traumatic.

The Sting (Operation) of Life

When I was in first grade, a tandem of bullies terrorized everyone on the playground. They would not let us swing or go on the jungle gym without their permission. Never mind that recess was set up by the school to give us carefree time to rid ourselves of excess energy. Taxpayers had bought the playground equipment for us to enjoy. The grass was there to keep us safe in case we fell from the bars. None of that mattered because Danny M. and Joel W. were big and mean. They had the power to keep us huddled away from everything recess was supposed to be.

Even though I didn't think they could really do it (they said they'd kill anyone who got on the equipment), I was afraid enough not to call their bluff. Of course, that power to kill us would only have been good for one time; after they ended one first-grader's life, they would be expelled from school—and those of us who had not been killed could go back to swinging and climbing. My reasoning told me that the hard part would be finding the sacrificial volunteer to get Danny M. and Joel W. to overplay their hand. Better yet, if we could find an adult who could impersonate a kid, then the bully buddies would not have enough power to carry out their enforcement scheme.

Perhaps my theological brother had influenced me more than I realized, but my solution for the playground was identical to God's sting operation. God provided someone over whom the enemy had no real power and used that volunteer to end the bully's threat once and for all. Jesus took upon Himself the form (disguise) of humanity in order to strip the enemy of his power over us:

> Since then the children share in flesh and blood, He Himself likewise also partook of the same, that through death He might render powerless him who had the power of death, that is, the devil; and might deliver those who through fear of death were subject to slavery all their lives (Hebrews 2:14,15).

Just as I had figured an adult would put an end to the bullies' reign of terror, so God used the life of His beloved Son to liberate us from the power of death. Death is the last foe before all of God's intended plan for the cosmos will be complete:

> But now Christ has been raised from the dead, the first fruits of those who are asleep. For since by a man came

death, by a man also came the resurrection of the dead. For as in Adam all die, so also in Christ all shall be made alive. But each in his own order: Christ the first fruits, after that those who are Christ's at His coming, then comes the end, when He delivers up the kingdom to the God and Father, when He has abolished all rule and all authority and power. For He must reign until He has put all His enemies under His feet. The last enemy that will be abolished is death (1 Corinthians 15:20-26).

What we have learned in this chapter is that we have two lives in two dimensions of the cosmos. As surely as we have had a physical body on Earth, so we will have a spiritual, or glorified, body in Heaven. Likewise, just as we have been able to function in this physical life even though we were dead in spirit, so we will be able to function completely in spirit when we are only dead physically.

In the next chapter we will look at what happened to Jesus when He died physically. His experience with life after death gives us our best picture yet of what it will be like for us when we die.

Notes
1. See Genesis 1:28.
2 See Revelation 20:13.
3. 2 Corinthians 5:1.
4 See Genesis 1:26
5. See Job 4:19; 10:9; 2 Corinthians 4:7.
6. See 1 Corinthians 15:49.
7. See 1 Corinthians 15:39-41.
8. 1 Corinthians 15:44.
9. See Luke 12:5.
10. See Hebrews 2:15.
11. Romans 6:23.

12. See Proverbs 14:12.
13. See Romans 5:12.
14. 1 Corinthians 15:56.
15. See John 8:24.
16. See Ephesians 2:1; 1 Corinthians 15:21.
17. Genesis 3:8.
18. See Romans 3:23; Ephesians 2:12; 4:18.
19. See John 5:24; Romans 4—7; Philippians 2:1-11; Colossians 1:13,14.
20. See John 3:15,16,36.
21. John 5:21.
22. See Romans 5:12-19; Hebrews 2:14,15.
23. Matthew 4:8,9.
24. Ephesians 2:2.
25. Ephesians 1:20.
26. Ephesians 2:6.

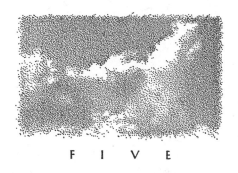

F I V E

LIFE AFTER DEATH

What happened to Jesus during His three days
in the tomb?

What is the difference between Hades and Hell,
Paradise and Heaven?

What is the Judgment Day, and what will happen?

Some people have a knack for storytelling. Their verbal images are so vivid that what they relate comes to life almost more than the event itself. With a perfect blending of humor, timing and narrative, they rearrange the details and sort the characters in ways that make everything clearer than if we were actually witnessing a scene firsthand. In fact, we would almost prefer to buy such a person a movie ticket, have him or her watch the movie for us and then tell us about it. Not only would they narrate the movie in great detail, but they would also give us a running commentary on their reaction—as well as that of the audience—to various parts of the movie.

Wouldn't it be fabulous if we could arrange to have someone else taste death for us? They could experience it on our behalf and then come back to tell us what it was like. Far better for death to be a secondhand experience than one we come to firsthand. Wouldn't it be great to know exactly what is going to happen the instant we die? Even if we couldn't have someone take our place in death permanently, it would still be fantastic to have a feel for what's going to happen when we leave our "earthly tent" behind.[1]

I suspect that's why many individuals are so anxious to read about other people's close encounters with death. Long tunnels, bright lights, sweet music, warm water, spirit figures, soothing voices—the list goes on and on in testimonies of people whose hearts stopped for several minutes—those who floated above themselves in the operating room or died but felt themselves drawn back to Earth for some purpose. That is really what we're interested in when we read a book like this one. What should we make of such stories and details? Where do we go and what will it be like after death? What does the Bible say about the instant we die? What does it mean to rise from the dead?

Earthly Risings

The Bible records several instances in which people came back to life physically on Earth after they died. Both Elijah and Elisha—two Old Testament prophets—prayed for young boys who had died, and those boys revived.[2] A similar episode takes place in the New Testament when Jesus prays for Jairus's daughter. Coming upon the stunned and confused mourners who are distraught at the death of such a young girl, Jesus tells the crowd not to see death as the final word. They laugh at Him until He raises her from the dead.[3]

Just as He reverses other seemingly permanent conditions on Earth (healing the blind, the paralyzed, the tormented, the sick), Jesus raises the dead to prove that He has the authority to change the way life is in this dimension of the cosmos. He overrides the consequences and conditions in which people have been forced to live. When the paralyzed man was lowered through the roof by his friends to get close to Jesus' touch, Jesus confronted and changed the man's physical and spiritual condition.[4] Jesus has the power to overturn our physical problems and meet our spiritual needs.

Other than Jesus' own resurrection, the best known of the biblical coming-back-to-life-on-Earth episodes is when Jesus calls Lazarus from the tomb. Lazarus's sisters were grieving over the permanence of death and wondering why Jesus had not done more to prevent Lazarus from dying. Mary even reproached Jesus for not caring more, for not helping more, saying, "If You had been here, my brother would not have died."[5] When the neighbors see that Jesus is moved to tears over his dead friend, they speculate on what He might have done to prevent the tragedy.

Although we can't say so with certainty, the likely cause of Jesus' weeping was not over the permanence of Lazarus's death.

Jesus said the "sickness is not unto [permanent] death, but for the glory of God."[6] It would seem that Jesus was weeping over the existence of death itself and all the wrong that death embodies. He promised Martha that her brother would rise again, but she misinterprets His words to only mean that her brother will rise on the Judgment Day. Martha and the rest of the mourners had no hope for any change in life's condition on Earth. That is why Jesus was deeply moved in spirit and was troubled. He came into the world to reintroduce God's (eternal) life to everyone now, and He wanted Mary and Martha to understand His resurrection power.

To demonstrate that He is "the resurrection and the life" and that whoever believes in Him will "live even if he dies,"[7] Jesus instructed the mourners to roll back the stone that covered the entrance to the small cave where Lazarus was buried. As if to say, "This is what God is like; this is what God can do in your life now," Jesus exclaims, "Lazarus, come forth!" Lazarus's earthly rising was a sign of the power of God. That is why Jesus told His followers that various signs—including earthly risings from the dead—would follow their proclamation of the gospel.[8] God can override the issues of our life's circumstances. That's the good news message Jesus came to Earth to proclaim.

Another biblical incident of earthly risings from the dead is often overlooked because it occurs in the midst of a far bigger saga. At the point when Jesus cried out and died on the Cross, the veil of the Temple was torn in two from top to bottom and a massive earthquake shook the whole region. The shaking was felt not only in the physical arena but also in the spiritual dimension. The ground split asunder, several earthly tombs opened and "many bodies" of those believers who had just recently died "were raised"; those people later appeared to "many" people after Jesus' resurrection.[9]

What do these earthly risings tell us about *life after death*?

The first thing we learn is that all of the people who came back to life on Earth eventually died again and stayed dead, physically. There is a great lesson for those of us who try to prolong our life on Earth—either by the way we live healthfully or by the extraordinary medical measures we take. No matter how many years we stay alive on Earth, we will eventually die and stay physically dead. Our ultimate hope, therefore, cannot be in an earthly rising or in a miraculous medical recovery. Such occurrences, though wonderful, only delay the inevitable.

It is also curious that the Bible is completely silent about the experiences these people had while they were dead—no mention of tunnels, soft lights or any other of the near-death happenings some people today claim to have. When people come back to life in the Bible, they do so not to tell about what it was like to die but to be testimonies of God's glory. The point is not what death is like but what God is like.

Near-Death Experiences

Death and near death are obviously very spiritual occurrences, but we should be wary of the spiritual experiences related to us by people who say they have died and come back to life. Though it is comforting to dwell on the inviting images shared with us about the moments right after death, those images can easily mislead us from the more profound truths about the life we can expect after death. The real issue is not what we will encounter in the brief moments when we pass out of the physical dimension into the second heaven, but what we will experience in the eons of eternity.

Stories that come from people's brush with physical death are at best distracting from what God wants us to know. At worst they are false and misleading. Scripture tells us to test spirits and their messages to make sure they align with the written Word of

God—the Bible.[10] In virtually every case where people "bring back" word from the hereafter, their message includes teaching that contradicts the Bible. Such information is not helpful to us even though it may seem to be when we hear it.

Before we take a trip to another part of the nation, we like to find out from someone what the weather will be like there. To be told to expect warm, sunny days is fabulous until we end up confronting cold, stormy weather on the trip. We should be careful not to presume that people know what they're talking about just because they make a confident claim on an issue we want to know more about. Our eagerness for information makes us vulnerable to deception.

There is no eternal solace and comfort, no real clue about our eternity, in the death experiences of anyone except Jesus Christ. That is why we will focus so much in this chapter on what the Scriptures tell us about Jesus' death and resurrection. Although His experience and activities in the grave are absolutely unique to Him and to God's purposes being worked through Him, they do give us intriguing glimpses into the life after death that each of us will experience.

JESUS' THREE DAYS IN THE TOMB

Only one person has ever come back to life without dying again. His name is Jesus Christ, and He made incredible claims about Himself and about what He was able to do on Earth as well as in Heaven. In fact, He taught His disciples how to welcome the will of God in the physical dimension through prayer by saying to God, "Thy kingdom come. Thy will be done, on earth as it is in heaven."[11] He made it very clear that His stay on the earth was temporary and purposeful: "I have come down from heaven, not to do My own will, but the will of Him who sent Me."[12]

Having come into the natural, earthly realm of the cosmos, Jesus told His followers that He would return to Heaven.[13] So if we're going to look for clues about our own death experience in the experience of someone else, that person should be Jesus. He is a true expert on Heaven and Earth, on this life and on the life to come.

Most of us are familiar with the Easter story—the Crucifixion, the burial in the tomb, the rolling back of the stone, the folded grave clothes and the exclamation, "He is not here, for He has risen."[14] But what about the three days when He was physically in the tomb? What was Jesus doing? What was happening to Him? What can we learn about our "after-death life" from what occurred immediately after Jesus' death before He ascended into the heavens?

To relate what was going on during those three days it is necessary to return to our discussion of the cosmos and in particular to a region within the spirit dimension (the second heaven) that we have not yet examined closely.

The Spiritual Nether World

Probably the most familiar term for this part of the cosmos is the "underworld," or the "netherworld." The word "nether" means lying beneath—down below as opposed to up above. The reason Holland is called The Netherlands is because so much of its land is below sea level. Unlike the Netherlands of the European community, the netherlands of the spiritual world is not a physical place, so it has no exact or actual geographic location. However, within the metaphoric view of the cosmos portrayed in the Scriptures, "above" and "below" signify relative proximity to "God Most High,"[15] who dwells within the "highest heaven."[16]

Because God is spirit, the realm of spirit (the second heaven) is closer to God than the natural realm of Earth. That is why the second heaven is above the earth, the sky and outer space. And yet many of the hosts of the spirit world—demonic powers and forces of wickedness—are in direct opposition to God. Hence, the spirit world also stretches below the earthly plane. In terms of its orientation, the netherworld is the extent of the cosmos that is the lowest or most distant from God's dwelling place in Heaven.

Upon death, Jesus descended into the spiritual netherlands—into "the lower parts of the earth."[17] Jesus told people that He would be going there, but they probably didn't fully understand what He meant, because they couldn't imagine the way that life after death really is. People back then were no more accustomed to thinking about what happens after death than we are today. Jesus said,

> For just as Jonah was three days and three nights in the belly of the sea monster, so shall the Son of Man be three days and three nights in the heart of the earth (Matthew 12:40).

The literalness of Jesus' descent into "the heart of the earth" can be troublesome to many people because the physical possibilities of going underground seem so remote and are difficult to visualize. Some people try to explain what happened to Jesus during His three days in the tomb in other more symbolic ways. But we should not forget that the entire scenario during those three days was played out on a spiritual plane of existence, not a physical, spatial one. Jesus had already descended from the "highest heaven" in the cosmos down to the earth, so to keep going down to a realm of the cosmos that was even more distant from God was not that extraordinary.

During the three days between His crucifixion and His (bodily) resurrection, Jesus' soul and spirit separated from His body (which remained in the tomb). His soul/spirit descended into the lowest spiritual "place" in the cosmos. Being without an earthly body was neither a new nor an alien experience for Jesus. He had only taken upon Himself the form of flesh and blood so that He might taste the experience of earthly death for all of us.[18] It was necessary for Jesus to go from Heaven to Earth and from Earth to the netherworld. His death in the physical realm had a specific spiritual purpose:

> Since then the children share in flesh and blood, He Himself likewise also partook of the same, that through death He might render powerless him who had the power of death, that is, the devil; and might deliver those who through fear of death were subject to slavery all their lives (Hebrews 2:14,15).

Because He had no sin, Jesus was not subject to the deadly repercussions of sin. The power of death obtained by the devil comes only as a consequence of a person's sin. This fact explains why Jesus could say that the devil "has nothing [on] Me."[19] Hence, if Jesus had not willingly chosen to lay down His earthly life, the devil would have had no authority to put an end to it. But that was God's plan, His commandment for Jesus from the beginning:

> For this reason the Father loves Me, because I lay down My life that I may take it again. No one has taken it away from Me, but I lay it down on My own initiative. I have authority to lay it down, and I have authority to take it up again. This commandment I received from My Father (John 10:17,18).

Jesus calls Himself the "good shepherd" because He sacrificed His life for the sake of giving life back to our spirits.[20] Through

His willing surrender, Jesus taught people for all time the meaning of true love:[21]

> Greater love has no one than this, that one lay down his life for his friends (John 15:13).

We can only marvel at the love of God "who did not spare His own Son, but delivered Him up for us all."[22] Not only does such a loving God "freely give us all [good] things," but He also made certain that we will always be able to be with Him. No power or host in any dimension of the cosmos will be able to return us to our previous state of spiritual death (separation from God):

> For I am convinced that neither death, nor life, nor angels, nor principalities, nor things present, nor things to come, nor powers, nor height, nor depth, nor any other created thing, shall be able to separate us from the love of God, which is in Christ Jesus our Lord (Romans 8:38,39).

Jesus died in order to nullify the power of death. He was the ultimate Trojan Horse—allowing Himself to die as a means of conquering death forever. In Homer's epic poem *The Odyssey*, the Greeks pretended to sail away from Troy in defeat, but they left behind a hollow wooden horse (filled with soldiers). To celebrate their seeming victory, the Trojans brought the horse inside the city gates. That night, the concealed soldiers climbed out of the horse and opened the gates for the Greek army to enter and sack Troy.

The process by which Jesus accomplished His incredible victory over death gives us some wonderful understanding about our life after death.

The "Place" Called Hades

The consequence of death, as we have seen, is that people are cut off from God and from the arrangements for life that He initially conceived for them. Therefore, in talking about death as an exiled condition of the soul/spirit, we are describing it as a spiritual "place" far removed from the presence of God—the netherworld for human spirits and souls. In the Bible, this "place" is called *Hades* (Greek), or *Sheol* (Hebrew). The terms are sometimes used metaphorically to represent death, destruction, trouble, or the grave, but Hades/Sheol is the location (or state of being) to which the dead go "down" beneath the earth.[23] According to Jesus, Hades was the place to which a person's soul and spirit went after death to await the final judgment of God.[24] It was a prison of sorts for the spirits of human dead.[25]

The dead are not unconscious, as though in some sort of suspended animation in a spaceship from science fiction. They are not alive in the physical dimension, but they can hear and respond in the spiritual dimension. Though the biblical details are somewhat sketchy, it seems that prior to Jesus' death and resurrection the spirits/souls of the dead dwelt in Hades/Sheol. It sounds incredible to our empirical and rational view of the world, but the Bible strongly suggests that Jesus went to the imprisoned, disembodied spirits/souls of the dead and "made proclamation" of the gospel to them.[26] Jesus, Himself, foretold that He would proclaim His message to people who had already died:

> Truly, truly, I say to you, an hour is coming and now is, when the dead shall hear the voice of the Son of God; and those who hear shall live. For just as the Father has life in Himself, even so He gave to the Son also to have life in Himself; and He gave Him authority to execute judgment, because He is the Son of Man. Do not marvel

at this; for an hour is coming, in which all who are in the tombs shall hear His voice, and shall come forth; those who did the good deeds to a resurrection of life, those who committed the evil deeds to a resurrection of judgment (John 5:25-29).

When we have an incomplete cosmology, thinking of Heaven and Earth as merely two locations instead of as multiple dimensions, we miss the significance of biblical phrases like "the lower parts of the earth" and "far above all heavens." Jesus descended from the third Heaven, where He was "in the beginning with God,"[27] to Earth where He functioned in both the physical realm and in the second heaven—the spiritual realm. In like manner, upon death He left the physical realm of the earth and continued to descend (cosmologically, not spatially) into the deepest, most anti-God reaches of the entire cosmos. In God's master plan to redeem us, it was necessary for Jesus to penetrate every dimension of the cosmos, from the heights of the heavens to the depths (lower parts) of the earth:

Now this expression, "He ascended," what does it mean except that He also had descended into the lower parts of the earth? He who descended is Himself also He who ascended far above all the heavens, that He might fill all things (Ephesians 4:9,10).

Setting the Captives Free

"Above" and "below" take on much more meaning when we grasp the totality of God's redemption of the cosmos through Jesus, who is now seated at God's "right hand in the heavenly places, far above all rule and authority and power and dominion."[28] Because Jesus was obedient to God, even unto death on the Cross,

Therefore also God highly exalted Him, and bestowed on Him the name which is above every name, that at the name of Jesus every knee should bow, of those who are in heaven, and on earth, and under the earth, and that every tongue should confess that Jesus Christ is Lord, to the glory of God the Father (Philippians 2:9-11).

Ultimately, then, the most important detail we learn about Jesus' death and resurrection is His triumph. Our hope for life after death rests completely with the absolute and all-encompassing victory He won on the Cross. But we can glean a few more thoughts about our own after-death life from other mentions of Hades/Sheol in the Bible.

We do not know many conclusive facts about Hades/Sheol, nor are we encouraged to spend lots of time trying to imagine what it is like. That's why some traditional understandings of the matters we are discussing may differ in how literally they interpret the Bible accounts. Take, for instance, the story found in Luke 16:19-31, of a man whose wealthy life of ease on Earth contrasts sharply with his life after death in Hades:

Now there was a certain rich man, and he habitually dressed in purple and fine linen, gaily living in splendor every day. And a certain poor man named Lazarus was laid at his gate, covered with sores, and longing to be fed with the crumbs which were falling from the rich man's table; besides, even the dogs were coming and licking his sores.

Now it came about that the poor man died and he was carried away by the angels to Abraham's bosom; and the rich man also died and was buried. And in Hades he lifted up his eyes, being in torment, and saw Abraham far away, and Lazarus in his bosom. And he cried out and said, "Father Abraham, have mercy on me, and send Lazarus, that he may dip the tip of his finger in water and cool off my tongue; for I am in agony in this flame."

But Abraham said, "Child, remember that during your life you received your good things, and likewise Lazarus bad things; but now he is being comforted here, and you are in agony. And besides all this, between us and you there is a great chasm fixed, in order that those who wish to come over from here to you may not be able, and that none may cross over from there to us."

And he said, "Then I beg you, Father, that you send him to my father's house—for I have five brothers—that he may warn them, lest they also come to this place of torment." But Abraham said, "They have Moses and the Prophets; let them hear them."

But he said, "No, Father Abraham, but if someone goes to them from the dead, they will repent!" But he said to him, "If they do not listen to Moses and the Prophets, neither will they be persuaded if someone rises from the dead."

Some people take this story to be allegorical; others think the "great chasm" is pictured between Heaven and Hades. Rather than referring to Heaven and Hades, this text seems more likely to be describing two sections within Hades. It is likely that Hades was divided into what we might call a lower portion, possibly called *katoteros* (literally "lower or lowest parts"), which kept unrighteous souls/spirits, and an upper part in which righteous ones were confined. Between these two portions of Hades, there was a great divide so that the souls/spirits of those in the lower region of Hades could not cross over to the upper. The rich man was in the lower part of Hades. Lazarus was in the upper portion.

When Jesus stormed the gates leading to Hades, He disarmed the forces of evil and made a spectacle of their powerlessness.[29] From the upper portion of Hades He liberated "a host of captives"[30] who were imprisoned by the power of death. He took those souls and spirits with Him into the heavens. That host of righteous men and women—as well as those people of faith in Jesus Christ who have died since His resurrection—are the ones whom the Bible calls the "great...cloud of witnesses surrounding us."[31] Some of those godly people of faith, whom Jesus liberated from Hades and who ascended with Him into the heavenly places, are mentioned in the New Testament as examples for us to follow.[32]

They are alive and conscious right now. Though we cannot see them or communicate with them, they are living testimonies to the power of "the author and perfecter of our faith" who is seated "at the right hand of the throne of God."[33] They are spirit, not flesh; where they once inhabited both the natural and spiritual worlds, now they live only within the realm of the spiritual.

The upper part of Hades/Sheol has been emptied through the death and resurrection of Jesus Christ. Everyone who believes in Him passes out of judgment and enters eternal life that will never be cut off from relationship with God nor from His kind intentions for us.[34] That is what Jesus meant when He said,

> For God so loved the world, that He gave His only begotten Son, that whoever believes in Him should not perish, but have eternal life. For God did not send the Son into the world to judge the world, but that the world should be saved through Him. He who believes in Him is not judged; he who does not believe has been judged already, because he has not believed in the name of the only begotten Son of God (John 3:16-18).

Jesus radically changed the makeup of the cosmos. His obedience to His Father's will enabled creation to be restored in as profound a manner as it was created. Jesus was the One by whom and through whom the worlds were made;[35] and He was the One by whom and through whom the world was redeemed.[36] Hades could not withstand the assault of the Son of God.[37] Although Jesus conquered death, the people in His Church will still die physically. However, our souls/spirits will not be held captive, exiled from God in Hades.

Jesus' obedience to His Father's will enabled creation to be restored in as profound a manner as it was created.

Death has lost its power to separate us from God or to keep us from the life He intends for us to have in the future.

We cannot understand our life after death without understanding the cosmos before Jesus' death. The spirit world has changed dramatically since His resurrection. And the change Jesus effected when He went to Hades/Sheol means that His followers will not descend to the lowest part of the cosmos like we would have done otherwise. That raises the question of where we will go. What other clues about our future can we find in the record of Jesus' death and resurrection?

The "Place" Called Paradise

If Jesus descended into Hades immediately after His crucifixion, what did He mean by saying to one of the two criminals who were crucified with Him, "Today you shall be with Me in Paradise"?[38] Did Jesus go to Hades or to Paradise? How could He have gone to both places? Some people who interpret Jesus' descent into Hades as allegorical use the promise to the criminal as a proof text. But there are several possible explanations for what Jesus meant that still support a more actual descent into the netherworld.

It seems reasonable that Jesus' invasion of Hades did not take very long, probably no more than a part of the first of the three days His body was in the tomb. The "rescue operation" He carried out was executed quickly and completely. Hence, Jesus said "today." Additionally, Jesus' emphasis is on the expression "with Me." Jesus' promise is about fellowship with Him. By the authority given to Him, Jesus was granting the repentant criminal eternal life,[39] which, as we understand it, means that life will never be cut off from the Lord. Only days prior to His crucifixion, Jesus prayed,

> And the glory which Thou hast given Me I have given to them; that they may be one, just as We are one; I in them, and Thou in Me, that they may be perfected in unity, that the world may know that Thou didst send Me, and didst love them, even as Thou didst love Me. Father, I desire that they also, whom Thou hast given Me, be with Me where I am, in order that they may behold My glory, which Thou hast given Me; for Thou didst love Me before the foundation of the world (John 17:22-24).

The spirit/soul of the criminal, along with the souls/spirits of the liberated captives, was led into the presence of God where there is "fullness of joy" and "pleasures forever."[40] This contrasted sharply with the place where someone without a relationship with God would have been headed after death—and where the other criminal went.

Seated with Christ in the Heavenlies

Because Jesus mentions the name of a "place" called *Paradise*, to which it is possible to go after death, let us look more closely at what He may have been referring to. The essence of paradise (garden-park, orchard, forest) is like a spiritual Eden, the "garden of the Lord."[41] Because the word "paradise" is not used that often in the Bible, there is some uncertainty as to exactly what and where it is. The best way to think about paradise as it exists now (prior to the end of time when we will go to the place called Heaven) is as a spiritual state enjoyed by the souls/spirits of the righteous. It is a spiritual condition more than a spatial location, but it is in the spiritual realm of the cosmos.

Paradise is best defined by the presence of God. Paradise is the third heaven. Wherever God is, is paradise. In the spiritual dimension, Hades/Sheol is the lowest, most distant "place" from God in which human spirits/souls abide. In a correlating manner, paradise can be viewed as the highest and closest "place" to God for the spirits/souls of the righteous.

Just as eternal life is best understood in terms of permanently restored relationship with God, so paradise can be defined as fellowship with Christ in the heavenlies where we are (in spirit) "seated...with Him."[42] When Stephen was martyred, he cried out, "Lord Jesus, receive my spirit!"[43] Until the day when Jesus returns to Earth at the *Second Coming*, the souls/spirits of the righteous are "at home" with Him[44] in a particular portion of the spiritual realm called the third heaven, or paradise. Upon death, the repentant criminal would begin to understand what the psalmist David knew of God as his Shepherd—goodness and mercy and restoration in the valley of death's shadow.[45] What a perfect picture of the mercy of God toward any who believe, even if they come to that faith at the end of their lives!

In one of the well-known messianic prophecies, God promises

not to abandon Messiah's soul in Sheol/Hades, nor to let His flesh "undergo decay."[46] That is why Jesus says of Himself, "I was dead, and behold, I am alive forevermore, and I have the keys of death and of Hades."[47] People who have been made righteous by the grace of God through their faith in Jesus no longer go to Hades.[48] Instead they go to paradise, the third heaven. Jesus has wrested the keys of death from the hand of the enemy and He has forever unlocked the prison doors of Hades.[49] Immediately upon death His followers go to be with Him where He is, beholding the glory God gave Him "before the foundation of the world."[50]

Learning what Heaven will be like is not merely a matter of listing its attributes as though it were a featured destination spot in a tourist brochure. People's natural disposition is to want to strip Heaven of its profound spiritual realities and turn it into a glorified theme park or an itinerary stop on our after-death voyage. Actually, it can get a bit uncomfortable to encounter the huge spiritual implications of what has happened in the invisible realm of the cosmos to make Heaven a possibility for a sinful people like us.

People's natural disposition is to want to strip Heaven of its profound spiritual realities and turn it into a glorified theme park or an itinerary stop on our after-death voyage.

But without understanding the spiritual side of the cosmos, the place called Heaven cannot be fully appreciated. Now that we've explored the dimensions and places of the existing cosmos, we are more prepared to answer another of the troubling questions about our future life after death.

The "Place" Called Hell

There is one last fact about Hades that will surprise most people whose primary images and concepts of Heaven or hell come from popular books or movies. Hades is not the same "place" as hell. Hades/Sheol is the realm of the dead, but it is not, as many people mistakenly believe, the same as the hell of eternity.

The primary Greek word for the place where people will spend eternity apart from God is *Gehenna* (named after a valley near Jerusalem), not *Hades* (possibly derived from the god of the dead, Aides). There is some overlap of usage and meaning between Hades and Gehenna, but the basic contrast between them is that Hades is only a temporary abode for the dead, while Gehenna is an everlasting place of existence for those who will remain separated from God.

It may be more helpful to describe both Hades and Gehenna as states of being, or conditions, under which souls/spirits will live out the eons of eternity, rather than as places. The most glaring condition of souls/spirits in either Hades or Gehenna is their separation from the life God wanted to arrange for them, *and from God Himself.*

At the present time in the flow of cosmic history, the lower portion of Hades has not yet given up its dead. It will not be emptied until right before the great Judgment Day when every soul/spirit who has been held in its confines will stand before the court of Heaven to be judged.[51] In solemn contrast to God's eagerness to offer people forgiveness of sin while they are alive on Earth is His purposeful intent to judge the people of the world "who did not believe the truth," after they have died.[52] As the Bible says, "It is appointed for men to die once and after this comes judgment."[53]

God's judgment is not random or arbitrary; it is based on the truth as it is revealed through the words of Jesus Christ. God "has given all judgment to the Son."[54]

And if anyone hears My sayings, and does not keep them, I do not judge him; for I did not come to judge the world, but to save the world. He who rejects Me, and does not receive My sayings, has one who judges him; the word I spoke is what will judge him at the last day (John 12:47,48).

God's purpose for sending Jesus from Heaven to Earth was not to judge and condemn people to death but to save them from the state of death in which they were already living. Through the sacrifice of Himself, Jesus was "manifested to put away [cancel, annul] sin."[55] Adam and Eve's sin already introduced the condition of death to our souls/spirits, and our own sin spread that deathly consequence.[56] Since it was our disobedience to God's words in the first place that caused the cosmos to spin out of God's intended arrangement, it is only through subsequent obedience to His Word that His creation can be fixed again. God wants us rescued:

For God did not send the Son into the world to judge the world, but that the world should be saved through Him. He who believes in Him is not judged; he who does not believe has been judged already, because he has not believed in the name of the only begotten Son of God (John 3:17,18).

Jesus is "the One who has been appointed by God as Judge of the living and the dead."[57] He will preside in judgment over what people have done on Earth.[58] This ruling will seal the eternal destiny of people's souls/spirits. That is where Hades and hell can best be distinguished. Believers in Christ are not judged; we are spared the verdict and sentence because our "life is hidden with Christ."[59] Our sins have been forgiven. Therefore, there is nothing for which to be judged:

> If we confess our sins, [Jesus] is faithful and righteous to forgive us our sins and to cleanse us from all unright-eousness (1 John 1:9).

> But He [Jesus], having offered one sacrifice for sins for all time, sat down at the right hand of God. For by one offering He has perfected for all time those who are sanctified."And their sins and their lawless deeds I will remember no more." Now where there is forgiveness of these things, there is no longer any offering for sin (Hebrews 10:12,14,17,18).

The Judgment Day

The Bible tells us that everyone else, those who ignored Jesus' words and offer of forgiveness, will be judged according to what is written in two books that will be read on the Day of Judgment.[60] One of the books is a simple record of every person's words, actions and reflections during his or her life on Earth. It will contain all the thoughts and intents of their hearts,[61] their motives and secrets[62] and all their hidden deeds.[63] When the por-tions of this book that relate to each individual are read before all the assembled hosts of the heavens and the earth, no one will be able to claim that he or she is a good person. Every mouth will be stopped[64]—not by force, but by sheer self-realization of each person's wickedness.

The other book will offer the dead who are still in Hades even less hope for eternity. It is called the *book of life*, and it is a simple roster of names without notation or commentary. In the book of life are recorded all the "righteous" who have become righteous through the shed blood of Jesus Christ and have aligned themselves with the purposes of God through the ages.[65] When people invite Jesus Christ into their hearts, their names are added to the book of life, and Jesus promises to "confess" them before the Father.[66]

Jesus told His disciples that having their names recorded in the book of life in Heaven is far more significant than the fact that demonic forces are subject to them on Earth.[67] Though spirit forces from the second heaven can and do affect our lives, nothing has greater weight in the eternal outcome of our souls/spirits than whether or not our names are recorded in the "Lamb's book of life."[68]

In many ways, the outcome of Judgment Day is a foregone conclusion. Because the righteous souls/spirits of the dead will be with Jesus in the heavenlies, Hades will not contain anyone who was righteous in their deeds (righteous through Christ's deeds) while alive on Earth or whose name is in the book of life. Consequently, all the souls/spirits still in Hades at the Day of Judgment will remain forever separated from God, in hell (Gehenna).

Hell is also called the "lake of fire" that "burns with brimstone,"[69] perhaps a symbolic picture of excruciating spiritual pain that is comparable to the physical pain of being burned. Jesus calls hell (Gehenna) "the outer darkness," meaning the furthest possible distance away from the light of God; in that "place" or "state" there will be "weeping and gnashing of teeth."[70]

Everything in the cosmos that is out of the ordered arrangement intended by God will likewise be removed from God's presence and thrown into hell, the lake of fire. This is known as the *second death*, the final "cutting off" of all evil and all wrong in the cosmos. Death will die. So it will have no future life with us in Heaven. In a giant housecleaning operation, God will reassert total dominion over the heavens and Earth. He will throw (the first) death, as well as Hades itself, into the lake of fire.[71]

As the temporary abode of the dead, Hades will no longer be needed when hell, the eternal realm of exile, is put in place. And since death—being separated from God and His arrangements for future life—is due to sin, there will be no death in Heaven, because there will be no sin there.

Contrary to one popular myth about hell, the devil will not be acting as the warden or tormentor of its confined souls/spirits. Rather, the devil himself will be banished and bound to that place where he, along with the false prophet, the Antichrist and all demonic powers "will be tormented day and night forever and ever."[72] Hades, death, demons and the devil meet their death in hell. Never again will they have the power to touch God's creation. They will forever be removed from God's life and from God Himself.

The same end awaits all people whose names are not written in the book of life. Life after death will be glorious for those whose names *are* written in that book. So a very big part of the answer to what your life will be like after death depends on you. The choice is between eternal life and eternal death—being with God forever in Heaven or being conscious and sentient but isolated from Him forever in the lake of fire.

Notes
1. 2 Corinthians 5:1.
2. See 1 Kings 17:17-24; 2 Kings 4:18-37.
3. See Mark 5:22-43.
4. See Mark 2:1-12.
5. John 11:32.
6. John 11:4.
7. John 11:25.

8. See Matthew 10:8.
9. Matthew 27:50-53.
10. See 2 Corinthians 10:5; 1 John 4:1-3; Revelation 2:2.
11. Matthew 6:10.
12. John 6:38; see also 8:42.
13. See John 16:28.
14. Matthew 28:6.
15. Genesis 14:19.
16. Psalm 68:33.
17. Ephesians 4:9.
18. See Philippians 2:6-8.
19. John 14:30.
20. John 10:11.
21. See 1 John 3:16.
22. Romans 8:32.
23. Numbers 16:33; Job 21:13; Isaiah 14:11; Luke 10:15.
24. See Matthew 11:22-24.
25. See 1 Peter 3:18,19.
26. Ibid.
27. John1:2.
28. Ephesians 1:20,21.
29. See Colossians 2:14,15.
30. Ephesians 4:8.
31. Hebrews 12:1.
32. See Hebrews 11.
33. Hebrews 12:2.
34. See Ephesians 1:1-12.
35. See John 1:3; 1 Corinthians 8:6.
36. See Romans 3:24; 8:18-22; Hebrews 9:12.
37. See Matthew 16:18.
38. Luke 23:43.
39. John 17:2,3.
40. Psalm 16:11.
41. Genesis 13:10, and see Genesis 2:8,10.
42. Ephesians 2:6.
43. Acts 7:59.
44. 2 Corinthians 5:8.
45. See Psalm 23.
46. Psalm 16:10.
47. See Revelation 1:18.
48. See Romans 4—6 and 10:1-17.
49. Revelation 1:18.

50. John 17:24; Ephesians 1:4; 1 Peter 1:20.
51. See Revelation 20:13.
52. 2 Thessalonians 2:12.
53. Hebrews 9:27.
54. John 5:22.
55. Hebrews 9:26.
56. See Romans 5:12.
57. Acts 10:42 and see 2 Timothy 4:1.
58. See 2 Corinthians 5:12.
59. Colossians 3:3.
60. See Revelation 20:11-15.
61. See Hebrews 4:12,13.
62. See Romans 2:16.
63. See 1 Corinthians 4:5,6.
64. See Romans 3:19.
65. Psalm 69:28.
66. Revelation 3:5.
67. See Luke 10:20.
68. Revelation 21:27.
69. Revelation 19:20; 20:15.
70. Matthew 8:12; 13:42.
71. See Revelation 20:14.
72. Revelation 20:10; see also Revelation 19:20; Matthew 25:41.

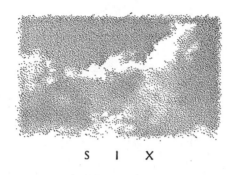

S I X

THE NEW HEAVENS AND EARTH

What does the Bible say about the end of the world?

What is the last trumpet, and when will it sound?

What will the new heavens and Earth be like?

Flying first-class is an entirely different world than flying coach. My whole family got to experience the "other" world a few years ago when we were taking a frequent-flier-miles vacation to Hawaii. I happened to be first in line at the gate counter when the agent announced the flight was overbooked. So I took a stab at the moon by suggesting a solution to their dilemma: "I have six seats in coach. How about upgrading us to first-class?" The agent smiled and replied, "Why not?"

For the entire flight, I kept telling the kids, "This isn't how life really is." But boy, did we enjoy ourselves! We were issued new boarding passes with new seat assignments as part of the upgrading process. Formerly, we were in rows 27 and 28 of the big jet (a right turn after entering the plane from the gangway). Now we were in rows 6 and 7 (a left turn). During the flight the attendants closed the curtain between the first-class cabin and the rest of the passenger cabin, so I didn't have much of a chance to glimpse our old seats until we landed and were exiting the plane. What a contrast of luxuries! I never found myself wishing for the "good old days" of coach-class. I never wondered what I might have missed by changing seats.

The "new" that God has in store for us in Heaven will be something like that contrast. We will not miss the old seats, and nothing of nostalgia will beckon us back to what was our place on Earth. This is the great promise of eternity. Life with God in Heaven is going to be so spectacular and so satisfying to the deepest longings of our souls/spirits that we can hardly grasp it.

The Enemy of our heart, the Liar of old, tries to rob us of our anticipation by filling our minds with questions inspired not by curiosity but by fear. We worry about what Heaven will be like, and we cling to the familiar trappings of this world because deep down inside of us we wonder if things are going to go poorly for us in eternity.

The prospect of first-class seats, instead of coach-class, is not an unnerving experience. Neither is shopping for new clothes (unless we can't find anything we like). When we know that the "new" is going to be better—more enjoyable, more attractive, more satisfying—than the "old," we look forward to it. I can tell you assuredly that the *new heavens and earth* will be far better than the old we have grown accustomed to in this life.

As we have been assembling the many puzzle pieces of what Heaven and life after death will be like, we've discovered there is much more to the picture than most of us realized. In order to fit all the pieces together we've had to expand our scope of study to include how God arranged the heavens and the earth in the beginning. The second heaven, or the realm of spirit, permeates the first heaven (the sky and outer space), as well as the earthly dimension of the cosmos. People are the only earthly beings who live in realms of both spirit and flesh. That is why we are the only earthly beings who have a life after our physical death.

God's ultimate plan is for us to spend life with Him forever in a "place" called Heaven. That is where we are headed. But we can't understand Heaven (as it will be) without understanding several other concepts that are usually missing in popularized notions of clouds, strumming harps and golden streets. We're like eager kids who keep asking, "Are we there yet?" But there's more to a trip than the arrival; there is a lot to see and experience along the way.

THE CREATED COSMOS AND TIME

Even though, like most fathers, I experience inexplicable bouts of grumpiness in the hours prior to a family trip, when the car needs packing, I thoroughly enjoy traveling to far-off places. I don't like the details of getting ready to go. I just like the traveling part. I like the feeling of driving down a stretch of road I've never been on before; I enjoy realizations such as, *So this is what Arkansas looks like!* The perfect trip for me would be a long train ride—like traveling on the Orient Express—where I could experience and learn things while I was heading toward an ultimate destination.

In the summer prior to my senior year of high school, my family moved away from our trellis-to-Heaven home. Naturally, I hated to leave my old friends and the familiar surroundings of my childhood home to live in a characterless new house situated in a desert town that boasted of enabling its inhabitants to "see the ends of the earth." Only once in the years since then have I gone back to visit my old home. I was shocked to see how it had changed: The lawn I used to tackle with a push mower every Saturday was nowhere near as steeply inclined as I remembered it; the place looked a bit more dilapidated; and the converted garage where my two brothers and I slept looked impossibly small. In fact, the whole neighborhood had changed. Where the alfalfa fields had been, shopping centers and homes and schools now stood. I hardly recognized anything.

I was not the only one affected by the passage of time. Though neighborhoods and cities do not show the change as readily as people do, the physical world around us is aging.

The cosmos itself is affected by time. It is wearing out. It is getting used up—not just in its natural resources like the ozone layer, fossil fuels, clean water and usable land. When death entered the cosmic picture through the sin of Adam and Eve, it introduced the beginning of the end. Entropy in the universe is more than just a fact of physics. It has far more spiritual than physical significance. It points us toward a culminating point in time when the worlds as we know them will no longer exist.

How ironic that most people think of the hills and the plains as "living forever" when our souls/spirits will long outlast such seemingly permanent parts of the physical cosmos. It is all part of God's plan for our future, and it is the last corner piece for our jigsaw puzzle of Heaven.

When the Bible tells us about God making the heavens and the earth, in the beginning, it is speaking only of the physical realm of the cosmos—outer space, the sky, the fields, the seas. The spiritual dimension of the cosmos already existed. God had already been "I AM" for the ageless eternity stretching back even further than such natural things as time and such physical particulars as space.[1] Jesus, too, was "in the beginning with God"[2] in the spiritual dimension:

> All things came into being by Him, and apart from Him nothing came into being that has come into being (John 1:3).

As the apostle John tells us, "The world was made through Him."[3] At the time when God spoke the physical worlds into being, the would-be Earth was "formless and void," like a wasteland.[4] It was an empty pocket of possibility, nothing but a blank emptiness in the midst of an exclusively spiritual reality. The Spirit of God brooded over that empty place, and God's commands created physical matter and natural life where no such substance or life-form had existed before. The tangible, visible world around us was actually brought into existence from out of the world beyond and above us.

Earth and the first heaven came into being after and out of the second heaven. This was accomplished by means of the spoken word of God. The natural, physical cosmos that seems to us to have such substance and permanence was fabricated out of the spirit realm:

By the word of the LORD the heavens were made, and by the breath of His mouth all their host. He gathers the waters of the sea together as a heap; He lays up the deeps in storehouses. Let all the earth fear the LORD; let all the inhabitants of the world stand in awe of Him. For He spoke, and it was done; He commanded, and it stood fast (Psalm 33:6-9).

By faith we understand that the worlds were prepared by the word of God, so that what is seen was not made out of things which are visible (Hebrews 11:3).

When Dirt and Trees
Coexisted with Angels and Righteousness

That early cosmos was quite different from the existing one. In the beginning, the physical and the spiritual worlds were far more integrated than they are today. The natural and the supernatural coexisted without much of a barrier or differentiation. Material substances like dirt and trees blended side by side with immaterial essences like angels and righteousness. That is why God could walk in the cool of the garden with Adam and Eve.[5] They could speak with Him, just as He was able to converse with them. So close was their interaction with God that when they sinned by eating of the fruit God had warned them against, in their naiveté they actually sought to hide from Him by going behind some bushes!

They had no awareness of His omniscience—knowing and seeing everything—because all their dealings with Him up to that point in time had been so intimate and immediate.

Their sin destroyed not only the close togetherness and relationship they had enjoyed with God, but it also drove a wedge between the natural and spiritual worlds in which they had been living. Because of their sin the visible sphere of Earth and of the physical heavens was mostly detached from the intangible realm of the spiritual heavens. The Garden of Eden was the place on the physical earth where spirit and flesh lived side by side; it was there that God breathed spirit into Adam's earthly frame and where He made a body of flesh to encase the spirit essence of Adam's excellent counterpart, Eve.

Spirit with flesh, flesh with spirit—that was the arrangement in the Garden of Eden before the fall of humankind. On the heels of the Fall, the earth was cursed and subjected to banishment from the close presence of God. It became primarily a physical world.

Eden was the perfect blend of spiritual pigment coloring a physical base. After the Fall, most of the spirit pigment was extracted, and we've been left to live in a world mostly comprised of just the base color.

It was like mixing paints—in reverse. A few years ago it was time to repaint the exterior of our house. My favorite part of the whole process was watching the clerk at the paint store add precise combinations of pigment to the base color to create exactly the hue my wife wanted me to apply to the walls and trim. It did not take much color to transform the base paint into a delightful shade of taupe. That is what Eden was like. It was the perfect blend of spirit and physical reality, spiritual pigment coloring a physical base. The heavens were totally integrated. After the Fall, most of the spirit pigment was extracted, and we have been left to live in a world that is comprised primarily of the base color. Little spiritual pigment still lingers in our world.

Adam and Eve's sin brought death to the heavens and Earth. It cut off the physical heavens and Earth from their source of spirit life and subjected the cosmos to certain decay. The world around us has been corrupted.[6] The ultimate ruin of the heavens and Earth was brought about by the power of Adam and Eve's decision to rearrange things in the cosmos to serve their desires instead of God's will.[7] Like little children who disobey their father's warning not to hold their newborn kitten so much that it cannot nurse, their selfishness was deadly.

NEW CLOTHES FOR THE COSMOS

The earth, the sky and outer space are wearing out. They are not eternal. They will not always exist. In their present configuration, they have no role in the eternity we will enjoy, because their corrupted nature sets them forever at odds with God's ordered and intended arrangement for the cosmos. Just as He spoke the existing heavens and Earth into being eons ago, so will He create a new heavens and earth in the future. God is eternal, and so is His word, but the present-day heavens and earth that were created by Him and His word ceased to be eternal when we reconfigured them through our sin:

> Of old Thou didst found the earth; and the heavens are the work of Thy hands. Even they will perish, but Thou dost endure; and all of them will wear out like a garment; like clothing Thou wilt change them, and they will be changed. But Thou art the same, and Thy years will not come to an end (Psalm 102:25-27).

God is going to recondition the cosmos. Because the heavens and Earth are getting old and wearing out, it will soon be time for the cosmos to change outfits.[8] Earthly clothing styles change so fast that no one but the wealthy can stay completely in fashion. But even normal people recognize when the time has come to adopt a new hairstyle, to wear shoes with a different-style heel and to permanently retire wide ties and leisure suits. We change our clothes at the end of the day because they have become dirty and smelly. The natural world has become worn out and sullied, made inexpressibly filthy because of sin.

Part of our fear about life after death comes from a misperception about eternal reality. People tend to think of this physical world as being permanent. It is the dock to which we want to keep our dinghy tied to keep from drifting away. The truth is that "[this] world is passing away";[9] anything that remains attached to it will share its fate. Jesus explains that the Word of God will surely outlast the heavens and Earth:

> For truly I say to you, until heaven and earth pass away, not the smallest letter or stroke shall pass away from the Law, until all is accomplished (Matthew 5:18).

Since Jesus Himself is the Word of God, the One by whom and through whom the worlds came into existence,[10] His words will outlast the existing cosmos, too. As He says, "Heaven and earth will pass away, but My words shall not pass away."[11] The heavens and the earth will pass away.

Their end will be cataclysmic and violent. The Bible tells us that everything in the physical cosmos will be shaken from its place in order to leave behind only the permanent, unshakable spirit world from which the temporary natural world was made:

> And His voice shook the earth then, but now He has promised, saying, "Yet once more I will shake not only

the earth, but also the heaven." And this expression, "Yet once more," denotes the removing of those things which can be shaken, as of created things, in order that those things which cannot be shaken may remain (Hebrews 12:26,27).

The Great Upheaval

The Day of the Lord will come as a culmination to a series of physical and spiritual happenings that are difficult to pin down in precise timing and sequence from the little we are told about them in the Bible.[12] Various images are used throughout Scripture to depict what will happen on that day when the (old) heavens and Earth are judged and destroyed. The stars will wither and fall from the first heaven like a fig tree casting its fruit, and the sky itself will be "rolled up like a scroll."[13]

It is difficult to imagine an earthquake large enough to be felt throughout the whole earth, but according to the Bible, such an upheaval—strong enough to move mountains and islands from their places—is coming:

And there was a great earthquake; and the sun became black as sackcloth made of hair, and the whole moon became like blood; and the stars of the sky fell to the earth, as a fig tree casts its unripe figs when shaken by a great wind. And the sky was split apart like a scroll when it is rolled up; and every mountain and island were moved out of their places (Revelation 6:12-14).

Growing up in California, I have experienced more than the average number of earthquakes, including being within a couple of miles of the epicenter of the 1971 6+ temblor in L. A., and the 7.1 Loma Prieta quake in 1989, which was centered not far from my home near Santa Cruz. When the Loma Prieta quake hit, I was driving on the freeway with a friend. Our car began to swerve and my friend thought we had a flat tire. I guessed earthquake right away and told him that in California, the odds are greater for an earthquake than for a flat. I have witnessed firsthand the power of such localized contractions of the earth. I cannot imagine the unleashed tumult when the entire globe will be gripped with life-ending convulsions.

Incredible heat will also accompany the end of the worlds. We are not told if such fire will come from the spirit realm, if it will simply be the result of fiery star-suns catapulting out of their places and plunging toward the earth or if it will be the inner upheaval of the molten core of our planet. The heat will be enough to melt every physical element in the cosmos. When the end comes, it will give rise to unearthly sounds of crashing and popping when the physical matter of the heavens and Earth collides and disintegrates. This fearsome picture is hinted at in several Bible passages, but none more clearly than that found in 2 Peter 3:10-12:

> But the day of the Lord will come like a thief, in which the heavens will pass away with a roar and the elements will be destroyed with intense heat, and the earth and its works will be burned up. Since all these things are to be destroyed in this way, what sort of people ought you to be in holy conduct and godliness, looking for and hastening the coming of the day of God, on account of which the heavens will be destroyed by burning, and the elements will melt with intense heat!

This passage tells us why the old heavens and Earth will be destroyed: God's wrath is directed "against all ungodliness and unrighteousness."[14] Because the old cosmos was unalterably polluted by sin, it will have to be done away with. God is a righteous God who will not allow unrighteousness to continue unchecked. It grieves Him to see the ways in which people corrupt His magnificent arrangement for the cosmos. He is going to put an end to the forces that ruin His creation. When gophers eat the roots of our garden plants again and again, we eventually take measures to stop them permanently.

Removing the Effects of Sin

When the end of the existing cosmos comes, it will be just like in the days of Noah—when people carried on in the midst of great wickedness as though nothing was wrong.[15] After only a few generations on Earth, humankind had done such violence to God's arrangement for life that He "grieved" over having creating them.[16] He decided to blot out our race and all other beings on Earth and in the sky—possibly to create another sort of being that would resist evil better than people do.

That was part of the tragic irony. God had given Adam and Eve stewardship of Earth and dominion over all its creatures,[17] so whatever corruption and evil developed in humankind spread to all living creatures by means of that God-given influence. Instead of being conduits of blessing to the whole earth and all its hosts, the earthly stewards of God's creation became carriers of deadly infection.

The sin and deathly separation introduced by Adam and Eve did not just affect human beings. The earth and its inhabitants were subdued by that same sin because it became part of the legacy passed on by the appointed rulers of the planet. That is why the hosts of the earth and of the first heaven were destroyed along with the people of the earth in the Great Flood:

Now the earth was corrupt in the sight of God, and the earth was filled with violence. And God looked on the earth, and behold, it was corrupt; for all flesh had corrupted their way upon the earth. Then God said to Noah, "The end of all flesh has come before Me; for the earth is filled with violence because of them; and behold, I am about to destroy them with the earth" (Genesis 6:11-13).

When the Flood was over, God promised never again to "curse the ground" on account of the evil in humankind's heart, nor would He destroy all creatures on Earth just because people went against His plans for how they should live. The "water of the flood" would never again cut off all flesh.[18] Rainbows in the sky remind us of that promise. This is what God pledged:

I will never again curse the ground on account of man, for the intent of man's heart is evil from his youth; and I will never again destroy every living thing, as I have done. While the earth remains, seedtime and harvest, and cold and heat, and summer and winter, and day and night shall not cease (Genesis 8:21,22).

"While the earth remains...." Even in the promise made long ago, God alluded to the eventual wearing out of the earth. In the existing cosmos, the ground has been "cursed" because of Adam.[19] Thus, the earth we live on is spoiled stuff. It is like cream that has gone sour; no matter how good the coffee is, it will be ruined if the bad cream is added to it. The curse on the ground means that the earth no longer provides for us on its own as God intended for it to do. Instead, we have to work and labor and fight against its accursed tendency to bring forth weeds instead of grain.

Every one of us has asked ourselves the cosmic question, Why do weeds seem to grow so easily while plants have to struggle to survive? The answer is the curse of Adam. Every year I fight a losing war with the small garden plot outside our living-room window. I get inspired (by my wife) to weed it and plant it—with

---

Try planting a pansy in the crack in your driveway where those weeds keep growing back and you will understand why God is going to replace the existing earth with a far more fitting one.

---

vegetables or flowers. The plants struggle to survive (not enough sun, soil that's too sandy) in the exact spot where weeds nonchalantly and arrogantly keep spreading themselves with utter abandon. The basic beauty of creation can still be seen and felt in the rivers, mountains and rain forests, but left to itself in an area that has been touched by human hands, the earth brings forth weeds more readily than fruit.

The earth has not lost all of its original nature to yield what is "pleasing to the sight and good for food."[20] However, the curse upon the earth means that we cannot live off the land without working, and unwanted plants generally outpace everything but zucchini in the garden. Such an earth is unsatisfactory for God's future plans for His children. Try planting a pansy in the crack in your driveway where those weeds keep growing back, and you will understand why God is going to replace the existing earth with a far more fitting one.

God's Judgment on Creation

The violent and catastrophic images of the end of the heavens and Earth are unsettling to us. That is understandable. We can hardly grasp the magnitude of such earthquakes and fire and disruption. The Day of the Lord is a terrifying thing, filled with "destruction from the Almighty" and "fury and burning anger."[21] It will be "a day of clouds, a time of doom,"[22] a "great and terrible day"[23] when "the sun will be turned to darkness, and the moon into blood."[24] But we should not forget that this judgment from God against the earth is part of His gracious plan on behalf of His children—those who want His will and His way.

His judgment is not indiscriminate. He is not messy or careless with His actions. In fact, that is what "judgment" means—an ability to decide between things. If we are facing surgery to remove a growth on our spine, we want a surgeon with lots of judgment, so that the growth and the spine do not get lumped together during the surgery. The doctor had better be able to tell the difference between the spine and the growth. God has the best judgment in all creation, so we who love Him and look forward to Jesus' appearing do not have to be unsettled or disturbed by the approach of the Day of the Lord. His judgment upon the world is for our sakes, to give us relief, not more to worry about:

> This is a plain indication of God's righteous judgment so that you may be considered worthy of the kingdom of God, for which indeed you are suffering. For after all it is only just for God to repay with affliction those who afflict you, and to give relief to you who are afflicted and to us as well when the Lord Jesus shall be revealed from heaven with His mighty angels in flaming fire, dealing out retribution to those who do not know God and to those who do not obey the gospel of our Lord Jesus. And these will pay the penalty of eternal destruction, away from the presence of the Lord and from the glory of His power, when He comes to be glorified in His saints on that day, and to be

marveled at among all who have believed—for our testimony to you was believed (2 Thessalonians 1:5-10).

Believers in Jesus Christ are not going to get caught up in accidental, collateral destruction caused by God at the end of time. This is not to say that bad things never happen to God's children. Life is filled with horrible tragedies befalling believers in Christ. Those who name Jesus as their Savior are subject to much of the same cruelty and random violence that come upon nonbelievers. Natural disasters, storms, wrecks and wars take the lives of "innocent" and undeserving Christians.

Rain falls on the righteous and the unrighteous.[25] Bad things happen to good people, and good things happen to bad people.[26] Such disparity is part of the fundamental futility of life beneath the sun, where sin has thrown everything out of balance. Listen to how the Bible describes the broken condition of our planet:

> The earth is broken asunder, the earth is split through, the earth is shaken violently. The earth reels to and fro like a drunkard, and it totters like a shack, for its transgression is heavy upon it, and it will fall, never to rise again. So it will happen in that day, that the LORD will punish the host of heaven, on high, and the kings of the earth, on earth. And they will be gathered together like prisoners in the dungeon, and will be confined in prison; and after many days they will be punished (Isaiah 24:19-22).

Thus, while it is true that a believer's car is as likely as a nonbeliever's car to be swept away in a rain-swollen river, it is not the case that both people are equally subject to the acts of God's judgment against sin at the end of the world. There is a huge difference between disasters that are the result of living on a broken planet under the curse of sin and purposeful retribution dealt by the hand of God upon that earth.

When Jesus tells of His future coming and how, on that Day, there will be two men working in the field and two women grinding grain, He makes it clear that God will take one and not the other.[27]

As discriminating as God will be between people in the Rapture, so He will be in dealing out His retribution. Two passages from the Bible confirm God's distinction of His people in the end:

> And I will display wonders in the sky and on the earth, blood, fire, and columns of smoke. The sun will be turned into darkness, and the moon into blood, before the great and awesome day of the LORD comes. And it will come about that whoever calls on the name of the LORD will be delivered; for on Mount Zion and in Jerusalem there will be those who escape, as the LORD has said, even among the survivors whom the LORD calls (Joel 2:30-32).

> Multitudes, multitudes in the valley of decision! For the day of the LORD is near in the valley of decision. The sun and moon grow dark, and the stars lose their brightness. And the LORD roars from Zion and utters His voice from Jerusalem, and the heavens and the earth tremble. But the LORD is a refuge for His people and a stronghold to the sons of Israel (Joel 3:14-16).

We are told that the fury of the devil against the human race will become greater as time draws to an end.[28] Through his henchmen, he will specifically target believers and seek to wear them down with every sort of affliction.[29] We do not know exactly what that will mean. But we can trust the Lord to keep us strong through whatever trials we face. The point is not that believers are guaranteed a painless, trouble-free existence, but that we escape "the wrath of God"[30]—a curse the devil will not escape in "the eternal fire which has been prepared for [him] and his angels."[31] We can be comforted by two other passages from Scripture that remind us of the Lord's dominion over any circumstances that the devil might try us with:

> Do not fear what you are about to suffer. Behold, the devil is about to cast some of you into prison, that you may be tested, and you will have tribulation ten days. Be faithful until death, and I will give you the crown of life (Revelation 2:10).

> And the God of peace will soon crush Satan under your feet. The grace of our Lord Jesus be with you (Romans 16:20).

Leading Up to the End

The ultimate reconstruction and complete renewal of the existing heavens and Earth will not take place until the final judgment when "earth and heaven [flee] away" from the presence of Him who sits upon the white throne, and "no more place [is] found for them."[32] By that point in the scheme of God's plan, the spirit world and the physical world will once again be so interconnected that our individual, personal existence will no longer be tied primarily to the physical world. We will be less in touch with our physical being than we are now.

Our souls/spirits will be the principal reference points of our being. Instead of seeing dimly into the spirit world, it is more likely that we will have a dim cognition of our physical surroundings.

As we come to the fullness of time, reality will progressively become more connected to the spiritual dimension from which the present heavens and Earth came. For us as believers, maturity is learning how to put away natural perceptions and reactions and to appraise things from a more spiritual perspective:[33]

> For we know in part, and we prophesy in part; but when the perfect comes, the partial will be done away. When I was a child, I used to speak as a child, think as a child, reason as a child; when I became a man, I did away with childish things. For now we see in a mirror dimly, but then face to face; now I know in part, but then I shall know fully just as I also have been fully known (1 Corinthians 13:9-12).

Remember that the entire physical cosmos as we know it today will cease to exist, but we will continue to live. The process of the world's destruction, therefore, will not harm us in the way we might imagine it would. Those of us who have put our ultimate trust in the Lord and who look forward to the new heavens and Earth will be awestruck observers of the end of the world, more so than victims in it.

When we watch a particularly intense movie with lots of scary action, we can get caught up in the emotion, and our adrenaline runs high as though we were in the movie. But no matter what happens on the screen, we are not in danger. Though it is not an exact parallel, I think it's close to what our experience will be when God ends the world. As the apostle Paul understood it, "the Lord will deliver [us] from every evil deed, and will bring [us] safely to His heavenly kingdom."[34] Notice, once again, that it is a heavenly, spiritual kingdom.

In the realm of spirit, nothing harmful can affect us once we have given ourselves completely to God. While we cannot lay claim to some protective buffer that will ward off every manner of calamity in our earthly existence, we can count on the security of our souls/spirits in His hands.[35]

He is a God of great grace, and we can be assured of His comfort and protection throughout the process of His judgment coming upon the earth. Just as He saved a remnant of Israel in the midst of their punishment for sin, so He will save us. This is the hopeful pattern that God has demonstrated throughout all time. He always saves a remnant.

Creation's Renewal

A second truth should bring us comfort when we think ahead to the Day of the Lord. Creation itself is eagerly looking forward to it:

> For the anxious longing of the creation waits eagerly for the revealing of the sons of God. For the creation was subjected to futility, not of its own will, but because of Him who subjected it, in hope that the creation itself also will be set free from its slavery to corruption into the freedom of the glory of the children of God. For we know that the whole creation groans and suffers the pains of childbirth together until now (Romans 8:19-22).

It may seem strange that Creation—the heavens and Earth—is excited about its own overthrow. But it knows something that we humans have a hard time remembering: It will be "reborn" and raised with a new "body." The perishable, natural creation will be transformed into an imperishable, spiritual cosmos, no longer tainted by the weakness and dishonor forced upon it by the sin of its human overlords, Adam and Eve.[36] The existing cosmos will be remade into a substance and arrangement that will make it perfectly suitable for all that God has in mind for eternity.

The New and Permanent Cosmos

So what do we know about the new cosmos? What will it be like, and how closely will it resemble the existing worlds? First, as we have already seen, it will last forever, enduring throughout all time.[37] The new cosmos is very much like the New Covenant that God established after the Old Covenant proved to be unsuitable for His plan to do humankind good all the days of their lives. Sin created an obstacle to God's longing to be with us forever, so He made a covenant with us that had provision to remove the cause of the separation:

> "This is the covenant that I will make with them after those days, says the LORD: I will put My laws upon their heart, and upon their mind I will write them," He then says, "And their sins and their lawless deeds I will remember no more" (Hebrews 10:16,17).

The Old Covenant could not do what God wanted to do for us permanently, so He made a New Covenant. Because of Adam and Eve's sin, we have had to sustain our physical life on the (old) earth by means of our labors and work. That was not God's plan for us. He intentionally made the earth so that it would bring forth good growth on its own. God was not looking for gardeners when He made Adam and Eve; He wanted fellowship with us, not work from us. Just as the (old) earth naturally produces weeds, so our (old) nature under the Old Covenant naturally produces unrighteous deeds. The New Covenant reverses that trend and supernaturally produces righteous fruit in us. The New Creation will, likewise, supernaturally bring forth righteousness without effort. In fact, righteousness will be one of its key elements:

> But according to His promise we are looking for new
> heavens and a new earth, in which righteousness dwells
> (2 Peter 3:13).

Unimaginable Joy

The Bible tells us about a second attribute of the new heavens
and Earth. The new cosmos will be filled with joy and continuous
celebration. The new order will be so different from the world
that we now know that we will have instant and complete com-
munication with God wherever we are, and formerly predatory
animals will graze side by side with those creatures that were
their prey on our earth.[38] While some people view these images as
metaphors for truths about Heaven that we cannot grasp with our
limited, earthly language, the reality about Heaven is that there
will be no evil and no potential for harm or disappointment. All
sorrow and every cause for "sighing will flee away" when the old
heavens and Earth retreat from before the presence of the Lord,
and "gladness and joy" will forever take their vacated places.[39]

It is almost as though the new heavens and Earth will be a
reversed mirror image of the old. Hence, God tells us not to think
about the new order of things in light of our earthly experience
now. For instance, God tells us that the deserts and wildernesses
of this life—those places in our physical world or in our personal experience where sin has blighted the life God intended—will
be transformed into well-watered places. This is not to say that
all deserts on Earth are bad, hostile places. When a desert is a
place of retreat and reflection, it affords great quiet and solace.
When, however, a desert is a "dry and weary land where there is
no water" and we long for the nearness of God like King David
did,[40] then we can see the contrast with Heaven.

Not a single confusing, taxing or troubling circumstance will exist in the new heavens and Earth.[41] Everything there will be, like in the Garden of Eden, to bless us and to do us good forever.

THE DAY OF THE LORD

At some future point in time, the thin veneer of the physical world will begin to peel away. With increased intensity, spirit-beings and powers from the heavens will intersect and impact the physical realms of the cosmos. These personalities and forces will cut into the world like searing heat through metal or like the sound of thunder rolling across a dark afternoon sky. These are not fanciful or imaginary. They are real and powerful but choreographed on a much larger life setting than we are used to thinking about.

Since our life after death is tied so closely with life after the old heavens and Earth pass away, we can find clues about our afterlife in the end of the world as we now know it. Though many people through the ages have tried to nail down an exact order and description for the events and players in the end times, an honest reading of the Bible does not really allow us to pinpoint the timetable for future occurrences or their aftermath with any accuracy. In fact, Christ explicitly warns us against such speculation.

The assignment Jesus gave His disciples was not to prognosticate about the end of the world, but to make disciples so that people would be saved from that eventual Day of the Lord. No one knows when that day will come, "not even the angels of Heaven, nor the Son, but the Father alone."[42] How one end-of-the-world happening relates to another, how exactly spirit forces will play out in human experience, we do not know with complete certainty. Such matters require an entire book of their own, and we do not want to lose sight of this book's purpose, which is to describe what our life will be like after death.

Nevertheless, we can identify one crucial event upon which everything turns: the second coming of Jesus Christ. When Jesus returns to the earth at the Second Coming, the physical heavens and Earth will suddenly experience the full reality of the realm of spirit that has been hidden from natural observation. When the moment comes, God "will bring with [Jesus] those who have fallen asleep."[43] Believers who are still alive on Earth at the moment of His return will leave behind their earthly bodies and join Christ in the realm of spirit "in the air," which is breaking in on the natural world.

The Sound of the Trumpet

What an incredible scene that will be when Jesus returns to the earth:

> But immediately after the tribulation of those days the sun will be darkened, and the moon will not give its light, and the stars will fall from the sky, and the powers of the heavens will be shaken, and then the sign of the Son of Man will appear in the sky, and then all the tribes of the earth will mourn, and they will see the Son of Man coming on the clouds of the sky with power and great glory. And He will send forth His angels with a great trumpet and they will gather together His elect from the four winds, from one end of the sky to the other (Matthew 24:29-31).

> For the Lord Himself will descend from heaven with a shout, with the voice of the archangel, and with the trumpet of God; and the dead in Christ shall rise first. Then we who are alive and remain shall be caught up together with them in the clouds to meet the Lord in the air, and thus we shall always be with the Lord (1 Thessalonians 4:16,17).

The second coming of Christ will be heralded by the blast of an angelic trumpet heard throughout the world all at once. "With a shout, with the voice of the archangel, and with the trumpet of God," the Lord will descend from out of the spiritual dimension into the physical world we inhabit.[44] His angels will be sent forth at the sound of that great trumpet, "the last trumpet,"[45] to gather the souls/spirits of righteous men and women who are the great "cloud of witnesses."[46] These include the dead in Christ whom God will bring with Him on that day.[47]

Every person will know instantly that this is the One whom God has chosen to be the "heir of all things,"[48] the One into whose hands all judgment has been given.[49] Throughout Scripture, trumpets herald specific events and messages. For instance, when God spoke to Moses and gave him the Commandments, an almost deafening reverberation of a trumpet spread through the sky, along with flashes of lightning and peels of thunder.[50] A great trumpet sounded in Israel to call the scattered and the perishing back to worship,[51] and a trumpet call also announced the reign of new kings. That is why Jesus will return to Earth accompanied by the sound of a trumpet.

When the final countdown to the end of the old cosmos begins, we will be made ready for the *future heavens and Earth* at the sound of the last trumpet. It is part of the wonderful mystery of our ultimate transformation. One of the most quoted verses in the Bible about our life after death speaks of the last trumpet:

> Behold, I tell you a mystery; we shall not all sleep, but we shall all be changed, in a moment, in the twinkling of an eye, at the last trumpet; for the trumpet will sound, and the dead will be raised imperishable, and we shall be changed (1 Corinthians 15:51,52).

We call it the last trumpet because of its place in the scheme of occurrences outlined in the book of Revelation in the Bible. The apostle John, who is granted sight into the spiritual realm, sees "things which must shortly take place."[52] The events of the end of the world begin to unfold. His vision is of a scroll fastened into short reading sections by means of a row of seven seals along its edge.[53] As the seal of each section of the chronicle is broken, John's attention is directed to various traumas and throes that are to come upon the earth and its inhabitants.

As mentioned earlier, these events underscore how utterly interconnected the spirit realm will be with the physical world. That is why the imagery of Revelation remains somewhat baffling to us at this time. Our physical world is not yet accustomed to such spiritual realities being so obviously manifested.

John tells us in Revelation that the opening of the seventh seal reveals a sequence of seven trumpets to be blown by seven angels.[54] When the first six trumpets are blown, John catches brief glimpses of the physical and spiritual forces that will be at work as the world winds down to its final annihilation. John hears trumpets that announce a rain of molten hail (8:7); a giant volcanic eruption that blasts a huge part of the earth into the sea (8:8); a bitter and deadly pollution affecting the earth's water supply (8:10,11); an onslaught of evil spiritual torments coming out from the abyss (9:1-11); and an invasion of spirit-born plagues upon the earth that kill one third of the population (9:13-19).

The Seventh and Last Trumpet

When the seventh and final trumpet sounds, it heralds the victorious reign of Jesus Christ over every natural and spiritual force in all of creation:

And the seventh angel sounded; and there arose loud voices in heaven, saying, "The kingdom of the world has become the kingdom of our Lord, and of His Christ; and He will reign forever and ever." And the twenty-four elders, who sit on their thrones before God, fell on their faces and worshiped God, saying, "We give Thee thanks, O Lord God, the Almighty, who art and who wast, because Thou hast taken Thy great power and hast begun to reign" (Revelation 11:15-17).

This trumpet call and what it announces is the key to our resurrection and to our life after death. Just as death came into the world through the sin of one man, so one man,[55] Jesus Christ, will completely banish death from the new heavens and Earth. He, Himself, is "the first fruits" of God's new order—a prototype for how everything in all of creation will once again be exactly as God intended it to be from the beginning.[56] When Jesus comes again to Earth, those who are His will become like Him[57] and be the next fruits of that renewed order.

> Then comes the end, when He delivers up the kingdom to the God and Father, when He has abolished all rule and all authority and power. For He must reign until He has put all His enemies under His feet. The last enemy that will be abolished is death (1 Corinthians 15:24-26).

The immense cosmic events we have looked at in this chapter can seem overwhelming and a bit off the subject that we're most interested in—namely, what our life will be like in Heaven. But simple answers about Heaven must come within the context of a larger framework. Having the whole jigsaw puzzle assembled gives added satisfaction when we fit some final pieces into place.

When I was a child living in Saugus, I wrestled, like most kids do, with the question most often posed to me: What did I want to be when I grew up? When I concluded that I wanted to be a cowboy, I had no grasp whatsoever of making a living or of a career. I knew nothing of mortgage payments, utilities bills, auto insurance, inflation or college. I did not know that the issue of my career was more complicated than just wanting to be something, and I didn't know what it would mean to grow up. Though I could gladly do without the bills I have to pay in adulthood, I much prefer the level of understanding I have now about life rather than the level of understanding I had in childhood.

Such is the puzzle picture we are trying to assemble about Heaven. The view we have examined about the nature and the destiny of the world we live in now enables us to finish the puzzle that depicts the place we call Heaven, where we will live forever. In the next chapter, we will look directly and specifically at Heaven, the most wonderful place in all the new heavens and Earth.

Notes

1. Exodus 3:14.
2. John 1:2.
3. John 1:10, and see Hebrews 1:2.
4. Genesis 1:2.
5. See Genesis 3:8.
6. See Romans 8:20,21.
7. See 2 Peter 1:4.
8. See Isaiah 51:6; 64:6; Hebrews 1:11.
9. 1 John 2:17.
10. See Colossians 1:16.
11. Matthew 24:35.
12. The Antichrist, the Second Coming, the Rapture, the millennium, etc.
13. Isaiah 34:4, and see Revelation 6:12-14.
14. Romans 1:18.
15. See Matthew 24:37,38.
16. Genesis 6:5,6.
17. See Genesis 1:28.
18. Genesis 9:11.
19. Genesis 3:17.

20. Genesis 2:9.
21. Isaiah 13:6,9 and see Joel 2:31.
22. Ezekiel 30:3.
23. Malachi 4:5.
24. Joel 2:31.
25. See Matthew 5:45.
26. See Ecclesiastes 7:15.
27. See Matthew 24:40,41.
28. See Revelation 12:12,13.
29. See Daniel 7:25.
30. John 3:36 and Romans 5:9.
31. Matthew 25:41.
32. Revelation 20:11.
33. See 1 Corinthians 2:14,15.
34. 2 Timothy 4:18.
35. See Ezra 8:31; Isaiah 41:10.
36. See 1 Corinthians 15:20-28; 15:44-49.
37. See Isaiah 66:22.
38. See Isaiah 65:17-25.
39. Isaiah 51:11.
40. Psalm 63:1.
41. See Isaiah 65:18-21.
42. Matthew 24:36.
43. 1 Thessalonians 4:14.
44. 1 Thessalonians 4:16.
45. 1 Corinthians 15:52.
46. Hebrews 12:1.
47. See 1 Thessalonians 4:14.
48. Hebrews 1:2.
49. See John 5:22.
50. See Exodus 19:16.
51. See Isaiah 27:13.
52. Revelation 1:1.
53. See Revelation 5:1 (See also Gary Matsdorf, *What Must Soon Take Place* [Kaneohe, Hawaii: Straight Street Publishing, 1996], pp. 57, 58.)
54. See Revelation 8:1-6.
55. See Romans 5:19; 1 Corinthians 15:21.
56. 1 Corinthians 15:20,23.
57. See 1 John 3:2.

THE "PLACE" CALLED HEAVEN

What will Heaven look like, and where is it located?

What will we see in the throne room of Heaven?

What will we do in Heaven?

And now we come to our destination, completing the jigsaw puzzle of Heaven. In this chapter we will look at Heaven from many different angles—describing some of its features, discussing specific rewards that await us there and examining what we will be doing in Heaven. The last leg of our journey will also involve a bit more discussion about some key events at the end of time that lead to the final establishment of the new heavens and earth.

When we realize that the existing heavens and earth are not exactly the same as the new heavens and earth, we have all the edges of our puzzle pieced together. The three existing heavens are each different from one another though often spoken of together. The first heaven is physical; the second heaven is spiritual. Just as the physical heaven has two fairly distinct parts to it (Earth's atmosphere and outer space), so we have studied a particular place within the entire second heaven, called the third heaven, or paradise. That is where God dwells, and where Christ sits at His right hand,[1] waiting for the perfect time for all things in the cosmos to be brought back into proper order.[2]

The night before His crucifixion, in the presence of Caiaphas the high priest, Jesus spoke words that for anyone else would have been blasphemy:

> I tell you, hereafter you shall see the Son of Man sitting at the right hand of Power, and coming on the clouds of heaven (Matthew 26:64).

He fulfilled His claim by ascending into the heavens.[3] After rising from the dead, He went to be with His Father in the third heaven. Upon our earthly death we will follow Jesus into the presence of God in the existing heavens:

So then, when the Lord Jesus had spoken to them, He was received up into heaven, and sat down at the right hand of God (Mark 16:19).

That place in the existing heavens is not the same as the place called Heaven in the new heavens and earth. This is where the bulk of the confusion originates regarding where believers' souls/spirits go after death. People jumble the cosmology of the Bible by lumping the first, second and third heavens together. And they muddle the chronology of the Bible by equating the present heavens and earth with the future heavens and earth.

Prior to the historic event of Jesus' death and resurrection, righteous people who died went to a different place (the upper region of Hades) than where they now go since His resurrection (paradise, the third heaven). In the same way, the souls/spirits of the righteous reside in a different place now, prior to Judgment Day, than where they will dwell for eternity in the age to come, after Judgment Day.

Heaven is more a place to understand than to describe. In fact, it is so perfect in every way that it is difficult to portray in just a visual snapshot. A still photo of a group of friends cannot reveal their personalities, their voices or any of the things we have come to know about them. We point to the photo and say, "Those are my friends," but we know a picture doesn't do them justice.

That is why the Bible doesn't paint an extensive picture of Heaven; such a picture would be too one-dimensional, too static and too limited to communicate all the depth and richness that awaits us. But there are some details about Heaven that are very exciting. So what does the Bible tell us about the place called Heaven?

A REAL PLACE

As we learned in the previous chapter, the present heavens and earth are going to be replaced by a perfected, newly created cosmos—the new heavens and earth. The most detailed description in the Bible of the place called Heaven comes in John's spiritual revelation from God that is found in the last book in the Bible, the book of Revelation. It is here that John describes in earthly terms many incredible particulars of Heaven.

Though constituted of dissimilar stuff, just as our glorified bodies will be composed of different substance than our earthly frames, the new cosmos will be as material and substantial and sensory as the old cosmos. Sky and soil and streets and banquet tables and crowns and music and light—all tangible and perceptible items—will exist in Heaven. The place we call Heaven, the place where we will spend eternity, is part of the new cosmos; but it is a place as real and substantial as any location on Earth today. Heaven is not a state of mind or an altered consciousness to be accessed through meditation, hypnosis, drugs or mental discipline. Heaven is not a mystical oneness with the cosmos, a collective memory of the race or a featureless idea like beauty or truth. Heaven is not in your mind or wherever and whatever you want it to be.

The inhabitants of Heaven will eat at the marriage feast of the Lamb,[4] described as "a lavish banquet...of aged wine, choice pieces with marrow."[5] In Heaven there are trees and rivers, gates that never close and celebrations.

Near the end of Revelation, John paints a portrait of God sitting on a great white throne. From His presence the old earth and heaven flee away.[6] The scene takes place in the midst of Judgment Day when John sees "the dead, the great and the small, standing before the throne" awaiting their judgment "from the things which were written" in the *book of life*.[7] This is when death and Hades and anyone whose name is not found written in the book of life are consigned to the second death in the lake of fire.[8] After Judgment Day, all spiritual forces of evil will be confined so that they have no power to affect or influence anything or anyone in the new cosmos.

John continues his vision with a startling detail:

> And I saw a new heaven and a new earth; for the first heaven and the first earth passed away, and there is no longer any sea. And I saw the holy city, new Jerusalem, coming down out of heaven from God, made ready as a bride adorned for her husband (Revelation 21:1,2).

When most people think about Heaven, they mistakenly presume that it will be in the sky, but that is because they confuse it with the spiritual dimensions of the existing cosmos, which as we have seen, are above the earth. The place called Heaven will not be above the new earth, it will be on the new earth.

There will apparently be no separation between the heavenly and the earthly in the new cosmos. Just as the two spheres existed as one in the beginning in Eden, when God walked with mankind, so they will be reunited in the new cosmos. And just like Jesus came to Earth long ago,[9] so will the kingdom of God come to Earth. Christ's coming to Earth was not symbolic; neither will His Second Coming be metaphoric. So there is little reason to doubt the literalness of John's prophetic description of Heaven coming to Earth.

The place where believers in Jesus Christ will spend eternity is actually a huge city named New Jerusalem. In the existing cosmos, this city is a particular location in the third heaven, just as California is a place in the United States. It is the "city of the living God," where myriads of angels dwell along with "the spirits of righteous men made perfect."[10] This "capital city" of the kingdom of God will emerge from the realm of spirit-only to be beheld and lived in by you and me in our glorified bodies on the new earth.

IN GOD'S PRESENCE

We will look at some of its landmarks and particulars later, but in this fantastic revelation of our future home, John hears a voice from the throne of God, telling him (us) the most prominent feature of New Jerusalem: God will be there!

> Behold, the tabernacle of God is among men, and He shall dwell among them, and they shall be His people, and God Himself shall be among them (Revelation 21:3).

As obvious as that may seem, it has huge meaning for us because God's dwelling place always signifies His choice of people. Throughout history God's covenant with His people has been a promise to give them a land in which to live (e.g., Eden, Israel) and a corresponding promise to live there with them.[11] That is the importance of the Ark of the Covenant, the Tabernacle and the Temple: God dwelling in the midst of His people. The New Covenant promises that the Holy Spirit will live inside of us.[12] Indeed, if we do not have the Spirit dwelling in us, we do not "belong" to God.[13] Our earthly bodies are called "temple[s] of the Holy Spirit"[14] because the Spirit of God inhabits our vessels of clay.[15]

The Holy Spirit becomes a pledge,[16] a promise of the great day when our clay will be dissolved and we will have new bodies in Heaven. Since our glorified bodies will be made of heavenly substance, we will no longer be vessels containing the Spirit. We, ourselves, will be distinct spirit-beings in whose company and in whose midst God will be ever present. Not only will we resemble Him in our character and in our fundamental make-up, we will be like Him and near Him bodily. We will "see Him just as He is," and we shall become like Him.[17] The "nearness of God" that has been our good on Earth will be complete in Heaven.[18]

As the voice continues to speak about the New Jerusalem, it proclaims that God will personally

> wipe away every tear from their eyes; and there shall no longer be any death; there shall no longer be any mourning, or crying, or pain; the first things have passed away (Revelation 21:4).

Grief, anguish, wasting sadness and hurt will find no room in Heaven, and neither will injustice, sickness, anxiety, want or anything that gives rise to outcries from our souls. Things and circumstances of this life that produce sighing or groaning from the depths of our hearts will be completely absent in Heaven. We will experience no disappointment, no brokenness, no "turning out wrong." Nothing will afflict or oppress us—either inside our minds or in our circumstances. We will have no mood swings! We will live on a perpetual and exhilarating high akin to the feeling we have now when we shout "Yes!" at a great victory—a clutch goal at the buzzer, a perfect coming together of all the plans on the day of a wedding.[19] Just like theme parks on Earth are arranged and decorated to bring delight to everyone, God will situate everything in Heaven to envelop us in constant wonder and appreciation. We will be glad all the time.

Since Heaven is the fullest expression of God's will and way, we should expect it to satisfy us as nothing else could do. We can be assured that Heaven will be a place of perfect fulfillment.

PREPARED FOR EACH OF US

I was a child the first time I ever heard Jesus' incredible promise:

> Let not your heart be troubled; believe in God, believe also
> in Me. In My Father's house are many dwelling places; if it
> were not so, I would have told you; for I go to prepare a
> place for you. And if I go and prepare a place for you, I will
> come again, and receive you to Myself; that where I am,
> there you may be also (John 14:1-3).

Of course I knew lots and lots of people would have reservations
for places in Heaven, so I wondered how we would all find our
new addresses. I pictured a massive convention with registration
tables just inside the big white gates of Heaven. After making it in
past Saint Peter, each of us would gravitate toward the appropriate registration line determined by the first letter of our last name
posted on the wall behind the tables. Once we reached the correct
table, our names would be checked off and we would be handed
a key and an address on a slip of paper. If the person behind the
registration table was not too harried, we might even be told
how frequently the buses ran to our sector of the celestial city.

Unlike my mother, who used to scour magazines for pictures of neat-looking rooms, houses and gardens, my childhood
imagination was fairly undeveloped when it came to picturing
the perfect house in which to spend eternity. I figured I would
know my place by the address on the curb. But Heaven has no
tract homes, no endless rows of condos. Each "place" is custom-
designed and built. We will not need an address to find our
home. Putting this concept in earthly terms, the moment we see
it, we will know it is ours because it will be exactly what our
soul/spirit always wanted.

In this life we have longings that are "too deep for words."[20] We have a desire to understand and to know things we cannot even name because they have no natural answer. That is what Paul experienced when he tasted paradise and was caught up into the third heaven. The subjects and the issues in that dimension of the cosmos were beyond earthly comprehension.[21] Yet throughout eternity we will be satisfied and filled and contented—not like the drowsy feeling on Earth after a big Sunday meal but a sensation of anticipation and accomplishment surpassing any such elation we have ever known.

The point is not so much to draw a detailed physical portrait of our heavenly neighborhood as much as to realize that Jesus personally prepares our place in Heaven. He has always been intimate and personal with us on Earth—knowing everything about us. Even

---

One of the biggest lies the devil foists upon people is that after death we will become "one with the universe"—merging our individual consciousness into the universal life force.

---

more so will He and our Father be with us in Heaven. We will not be featureless, nameless numbers within the vast multitude of fellow saints. In fact, when we arrive in Heaven we will each receive "a white stone, and a new name written on the stone which no one knows but he who receives it."[22] A great throng of people from every nation, kindred and tribe will gather there,[23] and each of them (us) will experience constant intimacy and profound relationship with the Lord.

God is not just a thought or an impersonal force in the cosmos. He is not some sort of positive energy or collective good or higher consciousness. The God of all Creation, and Jesus His only begotten Son, have distinct and knowable personas. They invite us to know them[24] and to love them.[25] God tells us to worship no other gods[26] because He wants us so completely and so personally for relationship with Himself.[27] The Most High God welcomes us as His children:[28]

> See how great a love the Father has bestowed upon us, that we should be called children of God; and such we are. For this reason the world does not know us, because it did not know Him. Beloved, now we are children of God, and it has not appeared as yet what we shall be. We know that, when He appears, we shall be like Him, because we shall see Him just as He is (1 John 3:1,2).

NOT JUST A FACE IN THE CROWD

As we have been seeing throughout our study of life after death, God's whole interest is in restoring our relationship with Him, which was lost when sin broke our worlds apart. Each of us in Heaven will know the Lord as we have been known by Him.[29] Any suggestion that Heaven will diminish our unique soul/spirit personas simply does not correlate with Scripture.

God does not want to mix us up with everyone else as though He were tossing a salad or blending the ingredients of a cake. He delights in us—who we are, who He made each of us to be.[30] Since before our births, throughout our earthly lifetime, God, Himself, has been at work in us "for His good pleasure."[31] He wants to enjoy each of us forever. He does not want to blur us together in some sort of cosmic collective.

One of the biggest lies the devil foists upon people is the idea that after death we will become "one with the universe"—merging our individual consciousness into the universal life force. That is not at all what the Bible teaches. Our uniqueness will not be lost in Heaven, it will be accentuated. We will not get lost in the crowd in Heaven.

As if to communicate how well God and Jesus know us, they have designed a "place" that suits us perfectly. Heaven will be perfect for us.

When my oldest daughter was a toddler, we went through the nightly bath ritual. Most evenings we discussed the temperature of the water: "It's too hot, Daddy." "No it isn't, darling, it's just right." Perhaps recognizing that she was not convincing me of the objective truth of her claim each night, she reverted to philosophy by saying, "It may not be too hot to you, but everyone has their own feel." It was hard to argue with that. One person likes hot weather and rising early to greet the dawn; another person would just as soon sleep the morning away.

There is no accounting for tastes. My kids love to drink orange juice for breakfast even when they have pancakes. Not me; the juice tastes too sour after the sweetness of syrup.

It is not usually a good shopping strategy for a husband to buy his wife a present that he would love to get. Socket wrenches or a new fishing reel probably will not do much to endear him to her. I've learned to listen carefully to the hints my wife drops about the sorts of things she likes. Once in a while she'll point out an entire store and tell me I could buy anything in it for her and she would be happy with it.

Longings Fulfilled

Such internal preferences enable us to have longings and desires. They provide us with fulfillment that is very personal and meaningful. When we receive a gift that suits our taste and our desire we exclaim, "Just what I wanted! Oh, thank you." The less it matches what we have been wanting, or with the style we like, the more we conclude that the gift was purchased out of obligation or habit, not out of affection for us personally. Politeness bids us thank the giver, but the nature of the gift and how closely it matches our preferences speak volumes about the nature of the relationship between the giver and us.

Certain religions of the world tend to view all desire and longing as inherently bad. Their goal is to rid themselves of such craving, which they believe is one of the main sources of human suffering. They believe the more that people can divest themselves of desire, the better the world (and their spiritual condition) will be. The biblical view, however, is that God invented desire and longing. He is the One who put such capacity in us so that He would be able to manifest His profound love for us. God delights in giving us the desires of our heart.[32] He wants to fulfill us and satisfy our desires in "scorched places" to such a degree that we can be compared to a well-watered garden "whose waters do not fail."[33]

The fact that we are encouraged to refuse fleshly, sensual and worldly desires should never be misinterpreted to imply that God wants us to be unsatisfied and emotionally impoverished. God does not want us to want the wrong things—things that corrupt and harm us[34]—but He made Eden and all of creation as places of great good and beauty, "pleasing to the [eye] and good for food."[35] That is why the Bible says, "No good thing does He withhold from those who walk uprightly."[36] The Bible encourages us to long for (among other things) what is right and good,[37] and gifts that will serve others.[38] *He wants us to long for Him.*[39]

This "imperishable and undefiled" future reserved for us—one that "will not fade away"[40]—was prepared before the foundation of the world.[41] Heaven will culminate everything God longed to give to us when He made the worlds and everything He has wanted with and for us ever since. In Heaven we will feel constant excitement and anticipation, like the buzz in the air we feel the night before a big sporting event, the eager waiting we go through for escrow to close on our dream house, the delightful prospect of a momentous engagement announcement. These are watered-down taste samples of a constant and intense flavor in Heaven. And yet, what we truly long for we will not even recognize until God perfectly satisfies those longings. Moment after moment we will look forward to being with the Lord and learning from Him.

THE CITY NOT MADE WITH HANDS

The Height and Width of Heaven

With John, we now catch our first glimpse of the city Heaven, the New Jerusalem, which shines with the glorious radiance of God:

> Her brilliance was like a very costly stone, as a stone of crystal-clear jasper. It had a great and high wall, with twelve gates, and at the gates twelve angels; and names were written on them, which are those of the twelve tribes of the sons of Israel. There were three gates on the east and three gates on the north and three gates on the south and three gates on the west. And the wall of the city had twelve foundation stones, and on them were the twelve names of the twelve apostles of the Lamb. And the one who spoke with me had a gold measuring rod to measure the city, and its gates and its wall. And the city is laid out as a square, and its length is as great as the width; and he measured the city with the rod, fifteen hundred miles; its length and width and height are equal. And he measured its wall, seventy-two yards, according to human measurements, which are also angelic measurements (Revelation 21:11-17).

To appreciate John's description, let's put it into earthly measurements. First of all, we see that it is staggering in proportions. Heaven is laid out in perfect symmetry, covering 2,250,000 square miles[42]—with each side of the walled city roughly the same length as the distance from Seattle to the midpoint of Baja California, or from Oslo to the island of Crete. In area it covers almost 65 percent of the continental United States. But the New Jerusalem is not a flat city.

From just inside each of the twelve gates of Heaven, the land begins an incredible ascent (at a 63-degree angle) for 750 miles until it peaks at the highest point, the mountain of God that extends 1,500 miles into the sky. That is more than 270 times higher than the 5.5-mile height of Mt. Everest. Suppose one of the gates of Heaven was located at a San Francisco beach. Geographically speaking, that would place the tip of the Mountain of God somewhere near Denver. What an unbelievable view each of us will likely have from our mansions! When John gives the astounding measurements of Heaven, he anticipates people's temptation to balk at such an incredible reality. It could be why he makes a point of saying that "human measurements are also angelic measurements."[43]

Truly, Heaven is the "city of our God, His holy mountain, beautiful in elevation, the joy of the whole earth."[44] This city and its mountain presently sit in the third heaven, from where the Lord answers our prayers.[45] Ezekiel refers to it as the "holy mountain of God" from which Satan was "cast...as profane" out of the presence of God[46] because he sought to "ascend above the heights of the clouds" and enthrone himself on the "mount of assembly" like "the Most High."[47] Just as the tabernacle built by Moses and the temple designed by David served as copies and shadows "of the heavenly things,"[48] so Jerusalem itself was situated on and around Mount Zion as a prototype of what would be true of the New Jerusalem:

And it will come about in the last days that the mountain of the house of the LORD will be established as the chief of the mountains. It will be raised above the hills, and the peoples will stream to it. And many nations will come and say, "Come and let us go up to the mountain of the LORD and to the house of the God of Jacob, that He may teach us about His ways and that we may walk in His paths." For from Zion will go forth the law, even the word of the LORD from Jerusalem. And He will judge between many peoples and render decisions for mighty, distant nations. Then they will hammer their swords into plowshares and their spears into pruning hooks; nation will not lift up sword against nation, and never again will they train for war (Micah 4:1-3).

Thus says the LORD, "I will return to Zion and will dwell in the midst of Jerusalem. Then Jerusalem will be called the City of Truth, and the mountain of the LORD of hosts will be called the Holy Mountain" (Zechariah 8:3).

So when the New Jerusalem descends from the new heavens to the new earth, it will fulfill one of the best-known descriptions of Heaven where no hurt will befall anyone on the holy mountain because "the earth will be full of the knowledge [of the glory] of the Lord":[49]

"The wolf and the lamb shall graze together, and the lion shall eat straw like the ox; and dust shall be the serpent's food. They shall do no evil or harm in all My holy mountain," says the LORD (Isaiah 65:25).

THE JEWELED CITY

Because the book of Revelation presents the reader with several symbolic images, and a vast array of beings and happenings that have no natural, earthly counterparts in our time, some people interpret the picture of the *heavenly Jerusalem* as an extended metaphor—not to be taken literally; hence, not that useful in describing what Heaven will actually be like. But as Wayne Grudem says, "It does not seem difficult to think that the description of the heavenly city...is a description of something that is real."[50]

The descriptions in Revelation convey the reality of our life after death, but they also point us to God's absolute perfection and glory.

Whether you are inclined to a more literal or a more metaphorical understanding of the scriptural portrayal of Heaven, the point is that God has prepared a place for us to spend eternity in His very presence. The descriptions in Revelation not only convey the reality of our life after death, but they also point us to God's absolute perfection and glory. Heaven is not just a place, it is the presence of God and of Jesus Christ, "the Lamb of God who takes away the sin of the world!"[51]

Our future home transcends earthly description. What Heaven will actually be like cannot come close to being fully rendered to us on the earth now. At most, what the Bible depicts of the place Heaven are sketches and brief glimpses, like pencil marks on a canvas that will soon be covered with oil paints and brush strokes.

Heaven is real but beyond our wildest expectations. For the brief snatches of eternity that we find described in the Bible we can be profoundly grateful, but when the city is finally and fully revealed, we will be wowed with its staggering dimensions and beauty. With that in mind, let us continue with Scripture's magnificent description of our future home.

The Wall

Details about the great and high wall stretching around the complete circumference of New Jerusalem—all 6,000 miles of it—make the dimensions of Heaven even more astonishing. This wall measures "one hundred forty-four cubits,"[52] an ancient standard that was equal to the length of a forearm. So the wall is approximately 200-250 feet tall. John does not describe its width, but we can assume its width keeps the wall from toppling over. The wall consists of jasper, probably meaning diamond. We cannot even begin to calculate the worth of such a diamond; the earthly measure of karats is meaningless on such a grand scale.

The Foundation

What rests beneath the wall of the city defies imagination almost as much as the diamond wall itself. John tells us that support for the wall comes from 12-layered foundation stones, consisting of different precious gems—sapphire, emerald, topaz and amethyst, among others. The 12 gates of the city are each carved out of giant pearls. That is where we get the expression "pearly gates." Unlike the gates outside of Disneyland that wait to open to the crowds each morning, the gates of Heaven never close because there is no night in Heaven, and there is no danger.[53]

Only those people whose names are in the book of life ever enter Heaven. They (we) are from every nation and from every people, the ones prophetically called the sons and daughters of God who come to the Lord from every corner of the world.[54] The walls of the city define its boundaries; they do not need to protect its inhabitants.

The River of Life

The 12 main boulevards running from the pearl gates to the mountaintop in the center of the city are divided roadways. Down the center of each of them cascades a branch of the "river of the water of life, clear as crystal, coming from the throne of God and of the Lamb."[55] The rush and swirl of that pure water, descending in a stunning series of varied rapids and waterfalls, is captivating and breathtaking. Once again we see how the actual, future place called Heaven, the New Jerusalem, fulfills Old Testament prophetic descriptions:

> Therefore we will not fear, though the earth should change, and though the mountains slip into the heart of the sea; though its waters roar and foam, though the mountains quake at its swelling pride. There is a river whose streams make glad the city of God, the holy dwelling places of the Most High. God is in the midst of her, she will not be moved; God will help her when morning dawns (Psalm 46:2-5).

The "streams" of the river bring rejoicing to the hearts of all the inhabitants of Heaven. At any point along each of the 750-mile-long roadways, the view of the river and the mist coming from it must bring the people of New Jerusalem refreshment beyond imagining.

On either side of the river grows the tree of life, which produces 12 kinds of fruit—one kind each month. Speaking of months, nowhere does the Bible say there will be no time in Heaven. Eternity is not timelessness; it is time without end. The tree of life not only gives satisfying fruit, but even its leaves have restorative, healing virtue in them.[56] The (old) earth was cursed because of our sin; the new earth will be in exactly the opposite condition. The very leaves of the tree of life enrich and endow the soil of Heaven as they fall to the ground and are absorbed into it. When the river spills forth from the gates of Heaven to water the whole earth, the fallen leaves will be carried to refresh the earth as well. Not only is the curse from Adam's sin gone in the new heavens and earth,[57] but it is also replaced with a double portion of blessing.

The Light of God's Presence

The streets of Heaven are made of purest gold, and so is the city itself.[58] When describing the gold of Heaven, John says it is like clear, or transparent, glass. This has led some people to dismiss the description of Heaven as purely symbolic because we have no such gold on Earth now. We should not forget, however, that the gold of Heaven is glorified just as our bodies will be glorified. If the splendor of our heavenly bodies surpasses that of our earthly bodies, it is not difficult to imagine that heavenly gold will be brighter and purer than earthly gold. When Jesus was transfigured on Earth, His heavenly garments became whiter than any earthly launderer could make them. Just because we do not have such gold on Earth should not lead us to conclude that the picture of Heaven is symbolic.

There are no streetlights, because the whole city will be illuminated by the radiance of the Lord Himself. We will not need candles or flashlights. The light from the sun will seem dim and dingy in comparison to the brightness of God's presence:

And there shall no longer be any night; and they shall not have need of the light of a lamp nor the light of the sun, because the Lord God shall illumine them; and they shall reign forever and ever (Revelation 22:5).

INSIDE THE THRONE ROOM

The images we glean from the Bible of God's throne room paint a picture of dimensions and beings that we cannot easily relate to on this side of eternity. If we try to interpret the picture too completely, we can lose sight of what we do know about the royal court where God has established His throne. God sits on a throne, "lofty and exalted" and from where He sits, the train of His robe spreads into the room and onto the floor.[59] Jesus sits at the Father's right hand, also on a throne.[60] Countless numbers of heavenly beings stand to the right and to the left of the thrones,[61] and one particular order of being, the four seraphim, seem to hover above the throne of God. The seraphim have three sets of wings: one set covers their face, one covers their feet and one is used to fly.[62] The four seraphim seem to serve as the primary worship leaders in Heaven, constantly declaring the holiness of God and announcing that the new earth is completely full of His holiness.

John describes more of the court:

There was a rainbow around the throne, like an emerald in appearance. And around the throne were twenty-four thrones; and upon the thrones I saw twenty-four elders sitting, clothed in white garments, and golden crowns on their heads. And from the throne proceed flashes of lightning and sounds and peals of thunder. And there were seven lamps of fire burning before the throne, which are the seven Spirits of God; and before the throne there was, as it were, a sea of glass like crystal; and in the

center and around the throne, four living creatures full
of eyes in front and behind (Revelation 4:3-6).

The Twenty-Four Elders and the Living Beings

We do not know exactly who the pictured elders are, but they may
be the 12 patriarchs of Israel and the 12 apostles of the church.[63]
Whatever their identity, their spiritual accomplishments on
Earth have given them a special designation and office in Heaven.
But when the four living beings who are before the throne lead
the host of Heaven in special praise, giving glory and honor and
thanks to God, the 24 elders fall down before the Lord, casting
their crowns at His feet.[64] However worthy they are of anything,
they know it is nothing next to the worthiness of the Lamb who
was slain. The elders carry two items that remind us of the most
meaningful activities on the old earth—a harp for worship and an
incense bowl filled with the prayers of the saints.[65]

The living beings immediately surrounding the throne are
the cherubim, possibly the highest order of celestial creature
because of the many biblical references to God being
"enthroned above the cherubim."[66] In a vision into the spiritual
realm, Ezekiel saw "in the expanse that was over the heads of the
cherubim something like a sapphire stone, in appearance
resembling a throne."[67] They are associated with the glory of
God, almost acting as couriers of His manifest majesty in the
heavens and in all the earth.[68] Outside of Eden, after the fall of
Adam and Eve, God "stationed the cherubim, and the flaming
sword which turned every direction, to guard the way to the tree
of life."[69]

The cherubim are multidimensional, multidirectional and
multifaceted beings unlike anything in our known universe. On
the one hand, their basic figure is that of a human, yet they also
resemble "burning coals of fire, like torches darting back and

forth" or "bolts of lightning.''[70] The cherubim are each accompanied by a "whirling wheel" and some sort of fire or burning coal flames between them.[71] Their form or manner suggests a gleaming "wheel within a wheel" that is able to move any and every direction without requiring that the cherubim turn to face the new direction.[72] In fact, they face in every direction at once, and they have four distinct countenances—of a lion, a calf, a human and an eagle.[73]

Both Ezekiel and Daniel describe the same flashes of fire that John sees coming from the throne of God.[74] These may be a picture of God's incredible power that is only barely contained and that manifests itself like a supercharged electrical generator, sparking and arcing with vivid sounds and lights. We can only imagine the raw energy that must emanate from the base of God's authority like miniaturized solar flares or like pulsating waves of electricity. The dynamic power of God that framed the worlds and raised Jesus from the dead radiates from the throne and stands ready to accomplish His word. What an awesome display of that creative and redemptive energy we will witness in Heaven!

The emerald-colored rainbow of suffused light around the throne softens the otherwise frightening flashes of fire and thunderous cracks streaking from the throne. In his vision of the same throne room, Ezekiel saw an "amber" rainbow,[75] perhaps alerting us that the rainbow changes color or is a yellowish-green. In either case, it signals covenant; the rainbow is God's sign of promise. After the Flood destroyed the earth, God promised to change the people of the world only through redemption, not annihilation.[76] The rainbow communicates that we are safe in the presence of our holy and all-powerful God because He is a God of love who made and will remake the worlds in order for us to be with Him forever.

The Golden Lampstand

The Holy Spirit is manifest in the throne room, pictured as the golden lampstand with seven lamps burning in front of the throne. Zechariah observed this same scene when he was told to prophesy to Zerubbabel: It is "not by might nor by power," but by the Spirit of God that mountains can be removed.[77] The seven parts of the lamp may be an allusion to aspects of the Holy Spirit who brooded over the formless earth eons ago and whose first act in our world was to bring forth light.[78] The Holy Spirit operates in the cosmos to give expression to the glory, the power and the personhood of God.

It may be that the Holy Spirit, Himself, is manifestly expressed in seven distinct ways—each being part of the whole person of the Holy Spirit. Such aspects of the Spirit of God might be compared to compounds or molecular structures of physical elements. For instance, water consists of oxygen and hydrogen; acetic acid has an empirical formula of CH_3COOH, indicating its composition of carbon, hydrogen and oxygen. The prophet Isaiah seems to identify seven spiritual elements or qualities of the Holy Spirit: wisdom, understanding, counsel, strength, knowledge, fear of the Lord and discernment.[79]

The Sea of Glass

In front of the throne and beneath it extends a large dais—a raised platform—of crystal that represents the absolute purity of the Lord. It is like a sea of glass upon which any blemish or sin would stand out in stark contrast.[80] A speck of dust would be noticeable, a finger smudge would be unthinkable. Imagine the footprints you and I would leave on such a pure landing if we had to walk there on our own righteousness. We begin to understand why the Bible tells us that no one is worthy enough or clean enough, on his own, to approach the throne of God across such a stainless dais:

For all of us have become like one who is unclean, and all our righteous deeds are like a filthy garment; and all of us wither like a leaf, and our iniquities, like the wind, take us away (Isaiah 64:6).

Such a picture of God's purity and righteousness makes other scriptures more meaningful. Through the cleansing work of Jesus' blood, we who believe in Him have unhindered access to the throne of God. Having offered one sacrifice for sin for all time, Jesus has inaugurated the New Covenant wherein God promises not to remember our sins. With that confidence, that we will not set off some heavenly alarm system, we can cross the dais to the throne.[81]

Continual Worship and Celebration

John's Revelation narrative describes the celebrative atmosphere and fullness of joy in the throne room:

And I looked, and I heard the voice of many angels around the throne and the living creatures and the elders; and the number of them was myriads of myriads, and thousands of thousands, saying with a loud voice, "Worthy is the Lamb that was slain to receive power and riches and wisdom and might and honor and glory and blessing" (Revelation 5:11,12).

This is no stuffy church service! Gratitude spontaneously overflows from people like you and me, who will fully appreciate just how great God's mercy has been to forgive us our sin. We will be standing there in the presence of holiness and power and truth that are beyond anything we can even imagine here on Earth. Unencumbered by the reluctance and the frailty of our flesh and old sin nature, we will be free to do what we were created to do—worship God Most High, the Ancient of Days, and celebrate His only begotten Son Jesus Christ, the Lamb who was slain.

The book of Revelation gives us numerous scenes of celebration in Heaven; and though not all of them can be set in an exact sequence of time, they give us an idea of what Heaven will be like when we worship:

And they [the cherubim and the twenty-four elders] sang a new song, saying, "Worthy art Thou to take the book, and to break its seals; for Thou wast slain, and didst purchase for God with Thy blood men from every tribe and tongue and people and nation. And Thou hast made them to be a kingdom and priests to our God; and they will reign upon the earth" (Revelation 5:9,10).

After these things I looked, and behold, a great multitude, which no one could count, from every nation and all tribes and peoples and tongues, standing before the throne and before the Lamb, clothed in white robes, and palm branches were in their hands; and they cry out with a loud voice, saying, "Salvation to our God who sits on the throne, and to the Lamb." And all the angels were standing around the throne and around the elders and the four living creatures; and they fell on their faces before the throne and worshiped God, saying, "Amen, blessing and glory and wisdom and thanksgiving and honor and power and might, be to our God forever and ever. Amen" (Revelation 7:9-12).

And the seventh angel sounded; and there arose loud voices in heaven, saying, "The kingdom of the world has become the kingdom of our Lord, and of His Christ; and He will reign forever and ever." And the twenty-four elders, who sit on their thrones before God, fell on their faces and worshiped God, saying, "We give Thee thanks, O Lord God, the Almighty, who art and who wast, because Thou hast taken Thy great power and hast begun to reign" (Revelation 11:15-17).

REWARDS IN HEAVEN

There is a reward for the righteous—not only in this life but also in our life after death.[82] Living the way God wants us to live in this life will lead us into direct conflict with the will and ways of a fallen world. Our choice to arrange our lives according to His order—remaining meek, hungering after righteousness, suffering persecution—brings us great reward in Heaven. If we conduct our life business on Earth "for the Lord rather than for man," we "will receive the reward of [our] inheritance."[83]

Eternal life in Heaven is the reward for our faith.[84] Whether we come to belief in the Lord Jesus Christ early in life or late, we will share equally in the reward of eternity in Heaven. That is the message of Jesus' parable of the vineyard workers and their wages.[85] Likewise, John's revelation from God tells us that those who overcome the world through their faith in Jesus will receive a common set of specific blessings; in Heaven we will

- eat of the tree of life in the paradise of God;
- be untouched by the second death—that place of eternal confinement for all forces of evil;
- eat of the hidden manna and receive a new name known only to us and to the Lord;
- live entirely in the light of Jesus, the Morning Star;

- be clothed in white garments and be acknowledged before the throne of God by Jesus;
- be granted permanent citizenship in Heaven, with identities bearing the personal signatures of our Father and of Jesus.
- be invited to sit with Jesus on His throne, just like He was invited to join His Father on His throne.[86]

Among other things, we will each receive a crown of righteousness,[87] a crown of glory[88] and one of life.[89] We will be invited to the great banquet celebrating our forever union with Christ,[90] and we will eat and drink the Passover meal with the Lord.[91]

If the vastness of the physical first heaven contains any indication of the magnitude of the new heavens and earth, we will be exploring and experiencing marvels of God's handiwork without measure. Since the physical and spiritual dimensions will be fully merged in the new cosmos, we will be able to actually live in the New Jerusalem but not be confined by the bodily limitations we encounter on Earth now, in the old cosmos. Will we have wings and fly about? Unlikely. But our raiment and mode of transport in Heaven will probably be more like that of God and His angels in the heavenlies now:

Bless the LORD, O my soul! O LORD my God, Thou art very great; Thou art clothed with splendor and majesty, covering Thyself with light as with a cloak, stretching out heaven like a tent curtain. He lays the beams of His upper chambers in the waters; He makes the clouds His chariot; He walks upon the wings of the wind; He makes the winds His messengers, flaming fire His ministers [angels] (Psalm 104:1-4).

Heaven is more than just relief and succor from this life. It is where we will experience the fullest release of our God-given potential and personhood. Nothing will obstruct His will for us. We will live out our highest destiny. We will find perpetual delight and blessing and wonder. The physical cosmos that stretches countless light-years away from Earth can seem to us in this life to be the epitome of unexplored marvels. All of us have wondered what it would be like to be transported to some far-off galaxy to see sights and learn things we could not know here on Earth. Multiply that sense and those distances innumerably and you will get the faintest taste of what we will experience in the countless days of eternity.

Imagine never needing to say good-bye to anyone. Think of what we will be capable of in our glorified bodies and consider the endless opportunities to meet and talk with fellow believers from throughout history. Though we do not fully understand all of the implications contained in the expression, we are told that we will be given a higher place in the heavenly order than that occupied by angels; we will "judge angels."[92]

And of course we will come to know more and more about the Lord. With each successive revelation of His character, His work, His holiness and His love, we will be able to praise Him without any weariness of body or mind. Our praise of Him will be so fragrant, so stunningly melodious, so full and rich that we will find it more satisfying than all the other things we do in Heaven.

TO KNOW GOD AND ENJOY HIM FOREVER

Most people have at least a small bit of concern that eternity will be somewhat boring. On Earth it is easy to equate "endless" with "monotonous," but nothing could be further from the truth.

Each moment in Heaven will be so vivid, so new, so full of wonder and life that we will live in constant amazement and awe.

I love to watch a major fireworks display. With each burst of the rockets, each stunning spray of muticolored flashes in the dark sky, I feel the momentum develop. I never tire of the next round of concussions and sparkling embers cascading into the night in varied kinds of symmetry and brightness. My favorite fireworks are those with an initial explosion of color and design, followed several seconds later with a second volley of flashes even more breathtaking than the first.

Such will be our continuous portion in Heaven. But we will see far more than staged fireworks. Beholding the Lamb of God on the throne—the One who gave His life as a sacrifice for our sins—we will experience ever more understanding of the richness of our restored relationship with God, our Father. What Jesus prayed for us on Earth will be perfected reality in Heaven:

> Father , I desire that they also, whom Thou hast given
> Me, be with Me where I am, in order that they may behold
> My glory, which Thou hast given Me; for Thou didst love
> Me before the foundation of the world (John 17:24).

That is the whole point of eternal life—knowing God and His Son.[93] In Heaven we will enjoy the culmination of everything that has been in God's heart for us.

When we consider both the magnificence of God's power and the eternity in which He has readied things for us in Heaven, we begin to grasp the magnitude of the delights awaiting us. It is no accident that God's Word tells us what we will experience in the presence of God: pleasures and fullness of joy.[94] In Heaven our worship and adoration of God will not come from faith (belief) in His words or hope in what He will do.[95] We will not be looking ahead, longing for more or better. All the delights and treasure of our entire earthly life could be contained in each *instant* of eternity in Heaven—which is why a thousand earthly years add up to little more than a day in Heaven.[96]

Our Hearts' Focus

For most of my Christian life, I have been struck with a particular detail about Heaven, which may serve to help complete our jigsaw puzzle—at least for now, here on Earth, as we await our final reward. In Heaven we will fall down in worship again and again. I do not picture millions and millions of us getting knocked over or tumbled about in disarray as though blasted by a strong wind. Neither do I envision a grand assembly of people engaging in formalized, ritualized, synchronized movements. What I imagine is something in between. The presence of God will be so immediate that there will be no need for an order of worship for everyone to follow. Each of us will worship spontaneously in direct response to every new revelation, every point of truth that we receive from the Lord.

Overwhelmed with each realization of just how wondrous God is in all His ways, we will stagger under a fresh "weight of glory"[97] that will cause us to drop to our knees or fall forward with our hands and faces to the ground. "O God, how great Thou art!" will be the cry of our hearts. As we begin to stand up to assume another posture of praise before His throne, we will receive another revelation that will send us to our knees again. Over and over and over we will learn of the mercies of our God. Again and again His wonders will be made known to us that we might sing His praises throughout all eternity.

Jesus Christ offers to each of us the opportunity to have our sin—what keeps us from relationship with God—forgiven by His sacrifice on the Cross. He died so that we might live forever. God so loved the people of the world that He gave His only Son, that whoever would believe in and put their trust in Him would not perish forever but enjoy eternal life instead. A new heavens and earth is coming. So, too, is Jesus' return and the Day of Judgment. The end of the world as we know it is already determined. When the final countdown begins, no one knows.

But the one thing we do know from the pages of the Bible is that God "desires all men to be saved and to come to the knowledge of the truth. For there is one God, and one mediator between God and men, the man Christ Jesus, who gave Himself as a ransom for all, the testimony borne at the proper time."[98]

Each of us must decide what we will do with the testimony of Jesus' life, death and resurrection. Heaven is the promise to everyone who acknowledges Jesus as their Savior and Lord. All who respond to the Holy Spirit's call with a simple prayer like, "Jesus, come into my life; forgive my sins; be my Lord," will one day witness this great scene in Heaven:

> And I looked, and I heard the voice of many angels around the throne and the living creatures and the elders; and the number of them was myriads of myriads, and thousands of thousands, saying with a loud voice,
>
> "Worthy is the Lamb that was slain to receive power and riches and wisdom and might and honor and glory and blessing."
>
> And every created thing which is in heaven and on the earth and under the earth and on the sea, and all things in them, I heard saying,
>
> "To Him who sits on the throne, and to the Lamb, be blessing and honor and glory and dominion forever and ever."

And the four living creatures kept saying, "Amen." And the elders fell down and worshiped (Revelation 5:11-14).

Notes

1. See Acts 5:31; Romans 8:34; Hebrews 1:3; 10:12.
2. See Mark 12:36; Hebrews 1:13.
3. See Acts 1:9-11.
4. See Revelation 19:9.
5. Isaiah 25:6.
6. See Revelation 20:11.
7. Revelation 20:12.
8. Revelation 19:20,21; 20:14.
9. See Philippians 2:5-8.
10. Hebrews 12:22,23.
11. See Ezekiel 36:27,28; 37:24-28.
12. See Romans 8:11; 2 Corinthians 6:16; 2 Timothy 1:14.
13. Romans 8:9.
14. 1 Corinthians 6:19; see also 1 Corinthians 3:16.
15. See 2 Corinthians 4:7; 2 Timothy 2:20.
16. See 2 Corinthians 1:22; 1 John 4:13.
17. 1 John 3:2.
18. Psalm 73:28; Isaiah 58:2.
19. See Isaiah 51:11.
20. Romans 8:26.
21. See 2 Corinthians 12:2-4.
22. Revelation 2:17.
23. See Revelation 7:9.
24. See Jeremiah 31:34; Hosea 6:3; Hebrews 8:11.
25. See Deuteronomy 6:5; 30:6.
26. See Exodus 20:3; Deuteronomy 5:7.
27. See Deuteronomy 5:9; James 4:5.
28. See Luke 6:35.
29. See 1 Corinthians 13:12.
30. See Psalms 100:3; 139:13-16; Ephesians 2:10.
31. Philippians 2:13.
32. See Psalm 37:4.
33. Isaiah 58:11.
34. See 1 Timothy 6:9; 2 Timothy 4:3; 2 Peter 1:4.

35. Genesis 2:9.
36. Psalm 84:11.
37. See Psalm 42; see also Philippians 4:8.
38. See Galatians 5:13.
39. See Psalm 42.
40. 1 Peter 1:4.
41. See Matthew 25:34.
42. See Revelation 21:16.
43. Revelation 21:17.
44. Psalm 48:1,2.
45. See Psalm 3:4.
46. Ezekiel 28:14-16.
47. Isaiah 14:13,14.
48. Hebrews 8:5.
49. Isaiah 11:9; see also Habakkuk 2:14.
50. Wayne Grudem, *Systematic Theology: An Introduction to Biblical Doctrine* (Grand Rapids: Zondervan Publishing House, 1995), p. 1161.
51. John 1:29; see also Revelation 5:6-13.
52. Revelation 21:17.
53. See Revelation 21:25.
54. See Isaiah 60:4-9; Hebrews 11:38; 1 Peter 2:4-12; Revelation 7:9.
55. Revelation 22:1.
56. See Revelation 22:2.
57. See Revelation 22:3.
58. See Revelation 21:18,21.
59. Isaiah 6:1.
60. See Ephesians 1:20; Hebrews 1:3.
61. See 1 Kings 22:19; Revelation 5:11.
62. See Isaiah 6:2.
63. See Luke 22:30.
64. See Revelation 4:9,10.
65. See Revelation 5:8.
66. 2 Kings 19:15.
67. Ezekiel 10:1.
68. See Ezekiel 10:18.
69. Genesis 3:24.
70. Ezekiel 1:13,14.
71. Ezekiel 10:6.
72. Ezekiel 10:11.
73. See Ezekiel 1:10; Revelation 4:7.
74. See Ezekiel 1:4,13; Daniel 7:9.
75. Ezekiel 1:28.

76. See Genesis 8:21,22.
77. Zechariah 4:6.
78. See Genesis 1:2,3.
79. See Isaiah 11:2-5.
80. See Revelation 4:6.
81. See Hebrews 10:12-22.
82. See Psalm 58:11; Luke 18:29,30.
83. Colossians 3:23,24.
84. See Romans 6:23.
85. See Matthew 20:1-16.
86. See Revelation 2:7,11,17,28; 3:5,12,21.
87. See 2 Timothy 4:8.
88. See 1 Peter 5:4.
89. See James 1:12.
90. See Revelation 19:7-9; Matthew 8:11.
91. See Matthew 26:29.
92. 1 Corinthians 6:3.
93. See John 17:3.
94. See Psalm 16:11.
95. See 1 Corinthians 13:8-13.
96. See 2 Peter 3:8.
97. 2 Corinthians 4:17.
98. 1 Timothy 2:3-6.

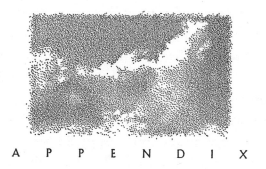

A P P E N D I X

COMMONLY ASKED
QUESTIONS ABOUT HEAVEN

Most of us have some of the same questions about Heaven and eternity. This book has come at those questions by giving a broad understanding of the cosmos, which God created and humankind altered. Within that large panorama, most of us want answers to a few other specific questions. If you're reading this section first, please know that the answers provided here will make much more sense to you after you have read the book, but they will provide enough information to satisfy your curiosity for now.

A caveat: We cannot pin down answers about Heaven if those answers are not given to us in the Bible. So perhaps this appendix should begin with the acknowledgment that it is with my understanding of the Scriptures that these questions are answered.

WILL I STILL BE "ME" AFTER DEATH?

There are two kinds of death—spiritual and natural. Death is not a state of oblivion or nonexistence; it is, rather, a separation from the life that was meant to be. Spiritual death cuts people off from relationship with God in the spirit realm, and our physical death will cut us off from relationship with the people we love here on Earth. Death is the state we are in after we have been cut off from the life we would have had and cut off from the people who love us.

Most of us learned years ago in science class that physical matter can exist in three states—solid, liquid or gas—without altering its fundamental organic composition. H_2O is a good example. It can be steam, liquid or ice. Water freezes to become ice; it boils to become steam. Steam will not quench thirst, water will not reduce swelling and ice cannot help remove wallpaper.

Each physical state has its own qualities, but each of them is H_2O. When we die physically, we merely change states. Our metamorphosis takes us from one form to another, from one dimension to another. Though we change states, we remain essentially who we are.

Our reborn spirit already exists in us in the same manner that it will exist after our bodies die. Even now our spirits inhabit the dimension to which we will be fully translated upon death. Though we are not that cognizant of our spirits in this present earthly life, and though our spirits will have new bodies in Heaven, they are fundamentally as they will be after death. We will simply be more conscious of our spirits in Heaven.

As we learned earlier, our souls are comprised of our thoughts, emotions, willpower and consciousness. Our awareness of the world around us, as well as of our inner selves, comes from the soul. The good news is that our personalities will be refined like gold from base ore, but who we are before we die is who we will be after we die. So our souls/spirits remain intact and essentially the same.

That is why birth is such an excellent analogy for death. As surely as a newborn baby "dies" from the womb-world into this world, so will our passing from life on Earth be a birth into another. Jesus said, "You must be born again."[1] Babies do not cease to exist when they pass down the birth canal; they just don't live in the womb any longer. The person in the womb becomes the person who lives in the world. The person in the world becomes the person who lives in Heaven.

Until we grasp this basic truth—that death is changed existence—we will stumble over what the Bible tells us about life after death. Our conscious existence will be extended, not exterminated. Our state will be transformed and we will shift dimensions, but we will not lose our identities:

Behold, I tell you a mystery; we shall not all sleep, but we shall all be changed, in a moment, in the twinkling of an eye, at the last trumpet; for the trumpet will sound, and the dead will be raised imperishable, and we shall be changed. For this perishable must put on the imperishable, and this mortal must put on immortality (1 Corinthians 15:51-53).

In our life after death, we will not become new (different) people. We will be ourselves, with the same fundamental qualities of personhood that we have now—minus any wrongs, distortions, wounding or bondage.

God calls Himself "I AM."[2] If this quality of being and remaining the same is so central to God's identity, then it makes sense that His children, made in His image, will always be who they are. When the offspring of "I AM WHO I AM" transition from the earthly plane to the heavenly dimension, their identities are not going to be "I am different than I was."

We are like expensive antique bureaus that years ago were finely detailed and hand-crafted by a famous woodworker. Since our creation we have been gouged by many things; we have been spilled upon, burnt by hot wax, water-stained and repainted in garish colors. Our hinges are loose, the drawers do not slide like they used to and one of our edges has been stripped of its molding. When such antique pieces get restored and refinished, they are not fundamentally altered; rather, they are renewed to what they have always been, despite the wear and tear.

The human soul/spirit is not immortal in the sense that it is not subject to death. Neither does the human soul/spirit exist as an eternal entity on its own. Only God, who has neither beginning nor end, is truly immortal and eternal.[3] He is never subject to death, change or dependence on anything outside of Himself. The human soul/spirit does not have an eternal nature of its own. God grants us eternal life, but we always depend on Him for our life in eternity, which is why Paul exclaims:

> Now to the King eternal, immortal, invisible, the only God, be honor and glory forever and ever. Amen (1 Timothy 1:17).

We will retain our original God-given personality and character when we rise from the dead. Everyone will live after death—either experiencing eternal death (separation from God and His life) in hell or eternal life in Heaven. We will all rise again; and though different eternities await us, depending on how we respond to Jesus Christ, we will exist forever—either with God or without Him.

WILL I HAVE A BODY?

The simple answer is yes! It will be a spiritual body—one that is far more appropriate for the new dimension in the new cosmos in which we will be living. It will be a body tailor-made by God, "eternal in the heavens."[4] Just as God formed our physical substance and frame in the womb and had a plan for our days on Earth,[5] so will He craft a spiritual body for us in the heavens. We are not our bodies—we are not our earthly bodily frame nor our future heavenly one. A body simply enables us to function in a dimension of the cosmos.

According to Jesus, it is intolerable for any spirit to be without a body-home.[6] Part of what makes us frightened about dying is that we do not want to be left unclothed, without a body.[7] Our uneasiness about whether or not we really will have a body, coupled with understandable curiosity, gives rise to the questions, What kind of body will it be? and What will it be like? The exact answer we would like to have to those questions is not given in the Bible. When we think of the sort of body we would like to have, we tend to think in terms of physical features. Our heavenly bodies are not described in the Bible, at least not their appearance or outward features. But we can surmise several facts about the bodies we will have after death.

Because we were made in God's image to begin with, most likely our heavenly bodies will resemble our earthly bodies in a glorified manner. This view is supported by Jesus' appearance after His resurrection. Before He ascended out of physical sight and into the (invisible) third heaven, His glorified body was similar to His earthly body. The main difference between His earthly and heavenly bodies was not in appearance but in capabilities. In His spirit body He could function in the earthly realm—speaking, walking, eating—but He also moved in the realm of the spirit— vanishing from sight,[8] walking through walls[9] and being received up into the third heaven.[10]

Several of the people who saw Jesus on Earth after He had risen from the dead thought He was a ghost, not a real person:

> But they were startled and frightened and thought that they were seeing a spirit. And He said to them, "Why are you troubled, and why do doubts arise in your hearts? See My hands and My feet, that it is I Myself; touch Me and see, for a spirit does not have flesh and bones as you see that I have." [And when He had said this, He showed them His hands and His feet.] And while they still could not believe it for joy and were marveling, He said to them, "Have you anything here to eat?" And they gave Him a piece of a broiled fish; and He took it and ate it before them (Luke 24:37-43).

One of His disciples, Thomas, who had not seen the resur-
rected Jesus with his own eyes, conjectured that the other disciples
had only seen a spirit. After Jesus appeared to all the disciples
again and allowed Thomas to touch the places on His body that
had been wounded by the spikes and the spear during the
Crucifixion, Jesus said to Thomas, "A spirit does not have flesh
and bones as you see that I have."[11]

Jesus had been functioning in both the earthly and the
spiritual realms throughout His life—walking on water and
being transfigured on the mountain when Peter, James and
John beheld Him conversing with Moses and Elijah.[12] When
Jesus was transfigured (metamorphosed), His whole being
became suffused with a radiance and brightness that was not of
this world.[13] Something of that glorious brightness will radiate
from our heavenly bodies, too. But Jesus still looked like Jesus.

The bodies we will have after death will not be made of flesh
and blood, but they will be stunningly more attractive than our
earthly bodies in the same way that flowers are more beautiful than
the seeds from which they come.[14] As opposed to being perishable—
like gallons of milk with expiration dates—our spirit bodies will
remain constantly fresh. Our heavenly bodies will never be getting
along in years, or getting old. They will be constantly renewed.

Earthly bodies develop toward maturity and then begin to
wear out. Aging on Earth is synonymous with wrinkling, stooping,
graying and growing increasingly feeble. No such process will
exist in Heaven. Earthly bodies, which encase the essence of our
personhood that God forms in our mothers' wombs, start very
small so that they can fit in wombs. Nobody gets born in
Heaven, so no one will need to be that young! We will all have been
made perfect (complete) in Heaven, and that implies maturity.

Our heavenly bodies will bear testimony to the truth about
God and His way. Our current bodies of flesh set themselves

against the Spirit and so often oppose God.[15] They carry the imprint of Adam and Eve's sin. Instead of being born in the dishonor of Adam's sin, our heavenly bodies will be living displays to commemorate Jesus' obedience. Our heavenly bodies will not fight against God's way; they will work for us to accomplish His plans.

On an especially positive note, our heavenly bodies will not lose steam late at night and they will not have trouble getting going in the morning. Here on Earth, "the spirit is willing but the flesh is weak."[16] Our earthly bodies are feeble, frail and susceptible to every manner of sickness and temptation. Headaches, a broken foot or a bout with the stomach flu quickly convinces us that our made-of-clay bodies are a force to reckon with. Our bodies resist, demand, expand and break down.

Our heavenly bodies, on the other hand, will be a miraculous power supply aiding us in our spiritual lives. They will be like fuel tanks or extra battery packs that actually add vitality to our souls/spirits, rather than depleting them.

Will I Go Into Suspended Animation When I Die?

As Jesus breathed His last on the Cross, He cried out, "Father, into Thy hands I commit My spirit."[17] His Father did not abandon Jesus at death; rather, He was reunited with Him. As we have already seen, Jesus was not in an unconscious state after death. He was not inanimate in the spirit realm, and He continued to do His Father's will after death as He had done before death. Though it was not in physical, bodily form that Jesus descended into Hades and made His proclamation of triumph over death, He was entirely conscious as He did His Father's bidding. You and I have no immediate assignment to carry out after our death because Jesus has accomplished it all. But we will be no less conscious after our physical death than Jesus was after His.

We will not be in a state of suspended animation after we die. The souls/spirits of believers in Christ join Him in the realm of spirit and become part of the "cloud of witnesses" that surround those of us who remain alive on Earth.[18] We do not need our earthly bodies to be conscious. In fact, we will be far more aware of the true reality than ever before. Instead of seeing dimly into the dimension of reality inhabited by God and the hosts of Heaven, we will get our first full glimpse beyond the veil. Just prior to an airplane's landing, most passengers crane their necks and look through the windows from side to side, hoping to get their first good view of the city where they are landing. We want to observe the place to where we have been traveling, even though we cannot see exactly where we will be staying once we actually arrive.

Death will afford us such a first panorama of eternity and the heavenly dimension. Until after we return with Jesus at His Second Coming to the earth, we will not yet reside in the place called Heaven. But we can say with certainty that when we die we will be with the Lord in the heavenlies.

Spiritually speaking, the Bible tells us that we are already there with Him in the spirit realm we call the heavenlies:

> Even when we were dead in our transgressions, [God] made us alive together with Christ (by grace you have been saved), and raised us up with Him, and seated us with Him in the heavenly places, in Christ Jesus (Ephesians 2:5,6).

In effect, we are now living in two places—on Earth and in the heavenlies—at the same time. That is a strange concept for us to grasp, but the places are in two dimensions. Light travels faster than sound. So we see lightning before we hear thunder. In other words, the light from the lightning bolt is already with us before the sound arrives. Light also travels much farther than sound. But if we are close enough to the lightning, we will eventually hear everything that we see of it.

While living in our earthly bodies, our souls/spirits groan in anticipation of our final release into the forever presence of God.[19] When we die we will be unencumbered with the bodies of flesh that are limiting—that are a barrier, holding back the sound of thunder from reaching where the flash of lightning has already gone. When that barrier is removed, there is nothing keeping us from the Lord. Scripture tells us that "to be absent from the body" is "to be at home with the Lord."[20]

> For we know that if the earthly tent which is our house is torn down, we have a building from God, a house not made with hands, eternal in the heavens. For indeed in this house we groan, longing to be clothed with our dwelling from heaven; inasmuch as we, having put it on, shall not be found naked (2 Corinthians 5:1-3).

When we receive Jesus Christ into our lives on Earth and have our sins forgiven, we come alive again in our spirits. Our relationship with God is restored, and every spiritual thing that had separated us from Him is removed. Once that new life with Him is established, nothing can separate us again. We will be with Him forever:

> For I am convinced that neither death, nor life, nor angels, nor principalities, nor things present, nor things to come, nor powers, nor height, nor depth, nor any other created

thing, shall be able to separate us from the love of God, which is in Christ Jesus our Lord (Romans 8:38,39).

Before Jesus' triumphant invasion of Hades, the devil had power and jurisdiction over people to keep them away from God because of their sin. The different dimensions of the earth and the heavens kept us distant from God, but we who were once far off, excluded from God and without hope, have been brought near to God through the blood of Jesus Christ.[21] That is the essence of true life; that is eternal life. When Jesus was raised from the dead, He was seated at the right hand of God "in the heavenly places."[22] After Jesus offered Himself as the once-for-all-time sacrifice, He sat down at His Father's right hand,[23] and we get seated with Him there.[24]

WILL I RECOGNIZE MY LOVED ONES?

God is the God of the living, not of the dead.[25] We do not cease to exist after death on Earth; we pass into the realm of spirit, but we retain enough distinctive essence of our true selves to be easily identified by everyone else. At the Transfiguration, the disciples recognized Moses and Elijah who had lived hundreds of years prior to Peter, James and John. Though the disciples had never met Moses and Elijah on Earth, they were able to recognize them for who they were. This has exciting implications for us. Not only will we recognize our friends and loved ones in Heaven, but it seems likely that we will also know all the other inhabitants, and everyone else will know us, too.

The Bible speaks of several distinct groups of redeemed people in Heaven, such as the "twenty-four elders,"[26] one hundred and forty-four thousand who go through the Tribulation with the Antichrist, and the great multitude that "no one could count, from every nation and all tribes and peoples and tongues."[27] Without recognizable bodies, these groups of heavenly residents would be impossible to identify, so it is safe to conclude that we will have features in Heaven to distinguish us from one another. We will recognize others in Heaven.

Here on Earth we know one another more than just by our looks. For instance, we converse over the phone with a voice, knowing it is our friend or spouse. Just by the sound of a person's voice we know who it is, and it doesn't seem the least bit odd to relate to that person without seeing a physical form. Likewise, when we read a letter from a dear friend, we actually read it with that person's voice echoing in our mind. We mimic the sound of it as we read the letter silently.

We get a feel for the people we know, a sense of their personality and humor and presence. When we happen to think of them, we can do so as easily in terms of personality (what they are like) as we can in terms of their physical features (what they look like). If you were to tell me that one of my golfing buddies went into a rage and broke the clubhouse window because of a missed putt, I would tell you there must be some mistake; my friends aren't like that.

My wife used to wear a blue and white ankle-length gingham skirt. I loved how it looked on her, just as I love particular outfits she has now. None of her clothes have lasted as long as our marriage. Different ensembles; same wife. When the clothes are bundled up in the bag she takes to the dry cleaners, I can recognize her dresses and blouses and say they are hers. But just because she's not wearing a particular outfit doesn't mean I have trouble recognizing her! So it will be when you and I put off our earthly outfit and put on our heavenly one.

When we dress up more than usual, people may exclaim, "Wow! I hardly recognize you." The transformation that takes place as a result of flattering clothes is somewhat akin to the transformation that will take place when we exchange these clothes on Earth for the tailor-designed outfits in the heavenlies. On Earth, only the rich and famous can afford to have personal tailors and clothes designers. When we go to be with the Lord, we all will have "custom" clothes.

We will be as distinctive in the heavenlies as we have been on Earth. The "cloud of witnesses" are called by name. They are not indistinguishable wisps of some ethereal, gaseous cloud. One of the biggest misconceptions about life after death is that we will simply fade into an impersonal cosmic whole and become one with a primal life force. Nothing could be further from what the Bible teaches. Jesus' heavenly state enabled Him to be recognized—though somewhat belatedly—by Mary, Peter and the others who knew Him before He was crucified.[28] The apostle Paul, who calls himself "untimely born" because he never met Jesus physically, says that the Lord (Jesus) appeared to him.[29] He knew it was the Lord when he saw Him.

Jesus' afterlife is the prototype and the pattern for ours. Though He left His physical body, He was not in a state of unconscious suspended animation after death. He was identified after His death even though His body was transformed and transfigured from what it had been before. We, too, will be changed enough to enable us to join the cloud of witnesses, but not so changed as to become unrecognizable or to lose our essential identity.

At a 25-year high school reunion, friends can still recognize one another despite the ravages of time. If the decaying influence of this broken world cannot erase the uniqueness of who God made us as individuals, then we should rest in the absolute assurance that our personhood will be enhanced and accentuated by God when we live in the new world to come.

HOW OLD WILL I BE IN HEAVEN?

Will everyone be the same age, regardless of their age at death on Earth? This is most often asked by mothers who have lost a child in the womb or very early in childhood. Understandably, parents want to know the nature of their future relationship with that child. Many mothers and fathers have been disallowed from carrying a child through infancy, enjoying a child for all the teenage years or developing the unique friendship that can form with their adult children.

Death has deprived us of so much on Earth! Even when we have enjoyed our children fully, we still taste a degree of death (impending separation) in the tears we cry at each graduation or wedding. Our hearts long to recapture the moments and the memories stolen from us by the thief, the prince of this world,[30] whose whole agenda is "to steal, and kill, and destroy."[31]

It is comforting to realize that one of Jesus' descriptions of eternal life is that it is abundant. Whatever measure of lost life and lost relationship has resulted from sin here, exactly the opposite (and even more) will be our portion in Heaven. The kind of affection and intimacy with family and friends that is so fleeting on Earth in the best of cases will be the "order of the day" in Heaven where time does not pass and we do not age. In this world we experience all sorts of loss—loved ones, careers, dreams, moments. In the life to come, loss will be unknown; regret, disappointment and second-guessing will not exist in any form.

In the tender book *I'll Hold You in Heaven*, Jack Hayford writes that parents who have lost an unborn child "will meet him or her someday and will simply 'know' who they are." After death we are not "airy ghosts floating somewhere in space." We can only speculate about the age and the features of such children as they will appear in Heaven. As Dr. Hayford continues, their appearance "is as unpredictable to you now as it was before [their] birth, but it is very possibly like the body his or her genetic code would have dictated had the child lived" on Earth.[32]

Though the Bible does not give an exact age for the inhabitants of Heaven, we will be changeless, like the Lord, and probably look like adults before they begin to age (on Earth). The earliest inhabitants of Earth, like Adam and Eve and their nearest descendants, lived hundreds of years.[33] Seth, who was Cain and Abel's younger brother, lived a total of 912 years. Did he look appreciably different at age 94 than he did at 612? A very long life tends to make one age look very much like another. Eternity makes age a moot point! Our heavenly bodies will be ageless.

WILL I BE MARRIED TO MY EARTHLY SPOUSE?

Another detail that Jesus mentioned about life in Heaven has caused some dismay among married couples. There will be no marriage in Heaven. At one point in Jesus' earthly ministry, some moralists (Sadducees) who did not believe in spirit-beings were trying to argue with Jesus against the reality of life after death. Their verbal strategy was to point out an inconsistency between the Bible and the possibility of people being alive in the third heaven after their death on Earth. God had instructed that when a man died, leaving behind no offspring to carry on his name, the widow should not take another husband from "outside the family" in her effort to keep the memory and name of her first husband alive.

When brothers live together and one of them dies and has no son, the wife of the deceased shall not be married outside the family to a strange man. Her husband's brother shall go in to her and take her to himself as wife and perform the duty of a husband's brother to her. And it shall be that the first-born whom she bears shall assume the name of his dead brother, that his name may not be blotted out from Israel (Deuteronomy 25:5,6).

Such a new husband would understandably want to have his own legacy in children. The solution was to have a brother of the first husband inseminate the widow in order to produce a son to carry on the name of his dead brother. The people arguing with Jesus were trying to make the point that such a guideline would not make sense in life after death. In the afterlife, whose wife would the woman be (in order to raise up a child) since she had been married to both of them on Earth? The same question might be posed in our culture: Because so many people have been married two or three times, to which of the earthly mates will they be married in Heaven?

Jesus' answer is that when people "rise from the dead, they neither marry, nor are given in marriage, but are like angels in heaven."[34] It is a meaningless argument to wonder which of the brothers would have the right to conceive a child with the woman in Heaven. No more people will be conceived in Heaven—period; the completed number of people will already have been reached. It is only on Earth that people are conceived in the womb. Only things of Earth can multiply by bringing forth offspring "after their kind."[35] Beings in the spirit world do not procreate. Hence, there is no commandment from God in Heaven to "be fruitful and multiply, and fill the earth."[36]

Jesus was not really commenting on the nature of the relationship between couples who have been married on Earth. He was correcting the people who thought they had figured out how ridiculous it was to believe in the resurrection of the dead.

We do not know exactly how we will relate to the other inhabitants of Heaven—except that there will be nothing in our connections with one another that relates to sexual union.

HOW MUCH TREASURE CAN I STORE UP IN HEAVEN?

One of the myths about Heaven concerns the matter of storing up treasures. Some people imagine a heavenly bank account from which they will be able to withdraw funds. Rarely does anyone think through for what reason they might need or want the money in Heaven. In New Jerusalem the streets are paved in gold, so there is no need for any savings account there. We will not need any money in Heaven. The idea of a bank account comes from what Jesus instructed His followers:

> Do not lay up for yourselves treasures upon earth, where moth and rust destroy, and where thieves break in and steal. But lay up for yourselves treasures in heaven, where neither moth nor rust destroys, and where thieves do not break in or steal; for where your treasure is, there will your heart be also (Matthew 6:19-21).

When we remember that the word "heaven" does not always refer to our eternal home in the New Jerusalem, but that it is often used for the spiritual dimension in the existing cosmos, Jesus' words have another more likely meaning. He was not explaining the investment plan for life in New Jerusalem. He was, instead, telling us that the material things we need for our earthly life are best secured through spiritual means. If we seek first God's will in our daily life, He will make sure that we have all the material things we truly need.[37] Anxiety and fear drive us to worry about our material life. Jesus was telling the people to make spiritual investments that would pay off on Earth.

What we invest in the spiritual realm is not subject to the corrosive powers of the physical realm.[38] The resources that God has are not vulnerable to earthly recessions or crime waves. When we pray for provision on Earth, we are asking to tap into some of what God has. In a metaphoric sense, treasure in the spiritual dimension is transferred to our account on Earth. It takes care of the rent or food or whatever the need about which we prayed.

By handling our earthly finances according to God's intended order (i.e., tithing, giving to others), we assure an adequate supply coming from the spiritual realm to us. It is not a formula that we can work; God is still the source from which all blessings flow. But the spiritual principle—like the last becoming first or the servant becoming the leader[39]—is one that Jesus wanted His disciples to know and live out.

Notes
1. See John 3:3.
2. Exodus 3:14.
3. See 1 Timothy 6:15,16.
4. 2 Corinthians 5:1.
5. See Psalm 139:13-16.
6. See Luke 11:24.
7. See 2 Corinthians 5:4.
8. See Luke 24:31.
9. See John 20:26.
10. See Mark 16:19.
11. See John 20:27.
12. See Mark 9:1-8.
13. See Mark 9:3.
14. See 1 Corinthians 15:37-49.

15. See Romans 8:1-8; Galatians 5:16,17.
16. Mark 14:38.
17. Luke 23:46.
18. Hebrews 12:1.
19. See Romans 8:22,23.
20. 2 Corinthians 5:8.
21. See Ephesians 2:11-18.
22. Ephesians 1:20; see also Colossians 3:1.
23. See Hebrews 10:12.
24. See Ephesians 2:6.
25. See Mark 12:27.
26. Revelation 4:10.
27. Revelation 7:4-9.
28. See Luke 24; John 20—21.
29. 1 Corinthians 15:8.
30. See John 12:31; Ephesians 2:2.
31. John 10:10.
32. Jack W. Hayford, *I'll Hold You in Heaven* (Ventura, Calif.: Regal Books, 1986), pp. 77, 78.
33. See Genesis 5.
34. Mark 12:25.
35. Genesis 1:24,25.
36. Genesis 1:28.
37. See Matthew 6:33,34.
38. See 2 Peter 1:2-4.
39. See Matthew 20:16; 23:11.

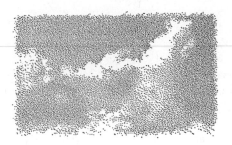

If you enjoy the way Daniel Brown translates spiritual truths into ordinary visual language, you may be interested in other of his written and audio materials, especially in the following categories:

• Personal Growth • Effective Discipleship
• Marriage and Family • What the Bible Says About...
• Local Church Leadership

Contact COMMENDED TO THE WORD (an extension ministry of The Coastlands) for these and additional resources by Dr. Daniel A. Brown.

Visit: www.coastlands.org
E-mail: ctw@coastlands.org
Fax: 831.685.3501
Phone: 831.688.2568